BUSINESS WRITING QUICK & EASY

LAURA BRILL

ama
com

AMERICAN MANAGEMENT ASSOCIATIONS

Library of Congress Cataloging in Publication

Brill, Laura.
   Business Writing Quick and Easy

   Includes index.
   1. Commercial correspondence—Handbook manuals,
etc. I. Title.
HF5721.B69   651.7'402   81-66216
ISBN 0-8144-5625-1   AACR2
ISBN 0-8144-7598-1 pbk

© 1981 AMACOM
A division of American Management Associations, New York.
All rights reserved. Printed in the United States of America.

First AMACOM paperback edition 1983.

CONTENTS

INTRODUCTION

If you're reading this book, you probably have problems writing business communications. Would it surprise you to know that most people feel varying degrees of discomfort when asked to compose a letter, memo, or report?

Speaking is a natural process; writing is not. We're exposed to spoken words almost from birth, but we don't get involved with serious paperwork until we're six or seven. Even in high school or college, we indulge in overwriting. Asked to hand in 1,200 words on a formal theme, we're likely to fill the page with 1,000 bits of padding.

The business person, armed with a thousand catch phrases, attacks the writing task by trying to sound important and wise. Since the reader's needs are barely considered, the letter may be unclear, pompous, or unfriendly. Still, the goal has traditionally been to do what everyone else does on paper.

What everyone seems to be doing isn't working, as many studies have shown. Part of the problem relates to the quantity of materials we're asked to read and the lack of clarity of the materials themselves. Part relates to old myths that are difficult to dispel. Evaluate these statements. Which do you think are workable truths?

1. The more advanced the executives you are addressing, the more impressive your writing should sound.
2. The more you write, the more impressive your writing becomes.

3. The most important goal in business writing is to capture and hold the reader's interest.
4. You should not use contractions (don't, isn't) or personal pronouns.
5. Readers are more responsive when you act important than when you sound friendly in your writing.
6. People are reassured when they hear familiar phrases.

Actually, none of these statements is true. Busy executives are more concerned with easy, quick understanding than with being impressed by your vocabulary. Simplicity, not quantity, ensures promotion. Although the reader's interest certainly counts, the most important goal in business writing is to get a message across, even if you have to sound boring. Contractions and personal pronouns have their place in business writing. Readers respond more favorably to a show of friendliness than to an air of superiority. Finally, keep in mind that people feel you don't care about them when you use tired phrases they've heard too many times before.

Here are some truths to replace the myths we've been taught about business writing:

1. Write the way you speak. Use simple, familiar language the reader can relate to.
2. Be reader-centered, not self-centered. This means showing more concern for the reader's understanding than for your own image.
3. Use a friendly, positive tone for letters. Avoid clichés and phrases that sound businesslike.
4. Write as little as necessary to get the job done. The only reason to write more is to make the reader feel good, not to make yourself look good.
5. Think about why you're writing before you begin. What do you want the reader to do, say, think, or feel in response to your communication? If you don't know, the reader never will.

Finally, think of your writing as part of a simple process. You set out to deliver a message. In turn, your reader, influenced by your word choice and the visual design of your page, chooses to respond to or ignore that message.

By the time you finish this book, you should understand how to make this process work for you.

1

SAY AS LITTLE AS NECESSARY

In the good old days, before mass communication muddled the mind and television addled it, quantity helped determine beauty in writing. Looking at those long, complicated sentences and weighty words, one might suppose that getting the message across was not a simple matter. Since the average person didn't read much that required urgent attention or exact understanding, the writer felt free to gratify what he considered a word-hungry public.

Today, with torrents of print flowing into homes and offices, no one has time to struggle with words. Either the message is understood quickly or it is not understood at all. Since the mind can absorb and relate to small doses of information better than to large doses, when your sentences get too long or your paragraphs too weighty, the reader tunes you out.

Studies of readability have shown that two elements affect reader comprehension. The first is sentence length. As a general rule, your sentences should average between 10 and 17 words. The more technical the work, the longer you can make the sentence. But if several consecutive sentences contain more than 14 or 15 words, you're in danger of losing your reader. The second factor is the number of syllables. Too many words of three or more syllables will make the reader shut you off, as if the strain is too great for one session. If more than 25 percent of your words are long and unfamiliar, you will not be easily understood. If you're writing for a wide audience, use as few long words as you can.

Certain words and phrases are considered prime cloggers. This means they crop up frequently in writing. Without them, a sentence can be shorter yet just as effective. This chapter outlines ways to eliminate clogging words and phrases.

WORDS YOU CAN LEAVE OUT

there—unless it's the subject, it can usually be left out.

> Weak: In the past, there were few politicians who could be trusted.
> Better: In the past, few politicians could be trusted.
> Weak: There will be three people attending the concert.
> Better: Three people will attend the concert.
> But: There are the two books you asked for.

it—don't use this in impersonal constructions.

> Weak: It is deemed imperative that we arrive on time.
> Better: We must arrive on time.
> Weak: It is the opinion of management that profits will rise next quarter.
> Better: Management believes profits will rise next quarter.

that, which, and *who*—leave them out when no misunderstanding would result.

> We think [that] shorter sentences are more effective.
> The agreement [which or that] we signed runs for five years.
> Mary Stone, [who is] my neighbor, works here.

Exercise
Remove unnecessary use of *there, it, who, that,* and *which.*

1. The report which [or that] you promised to send hasn't come.
2. It is probable that women managers must overcome prejudice.

3. There were several good ideas presented at the meeting.
4. It is expected that profits will be higher this year.
5. It is our president's view that the policy is sound.
6. Simon Green, who is our department's brightest new worker, won't be here much longer.

Possible corrections

1. The report you promised to send hasn't come.
2. Women managers probably must overcome some prejudice.
3. Several good ideas were presented at the meeting.
4. We expect profits to be higher this year.
5. Our president thinks the policy is sound.
6. Simon Green, our department's brightest new worker, won't be here much longer.

In all corrections, put in as much information as you consider necessary.

Intensives

Can a person be slightly pregnant or a little dead? Realistically, no. Some words shouldn't be intensified. For example, if you're the best, being the very best doesn't add anything to your state. If a task is impossible, you won't change it by making it very or highly impossible. In fact, you will only clutter your writing and contaminate the language. You weaken a word when you qualify it. How strong can "essential" be if you have to precede it with "absolutely"?

Don't overuse *very, definitely, absolutely, completely,* or *highly.* Never use them with these words: *unique, impossible, superb, superior, excellent.*

Illustrations

The product was *totally* unique. (Since unique means "one of a kind," how can the product be totally "one of a kind"?)

That statement is *definitely* incorrect. (Was there a question that it might be vaguely incorrect?)

The secretary was *completely* exhausted by the time she finished the minutes. (As opposed to a little bit exhausted? Think about what the word means.)

Repetition and Redundancy

When we repeat the same word or the same idea, it usually means we don't have much of importance to say. The only reason to repeat is for emphasis; otherwise, say it once and in only one way.

Common examples:

Don't say	*Do say*
each and every	each
first and foremost	foremost
one and only	only
total, complete	total
close proximity	near
consensus of opinion	consensus

Don't repeat words and phrases in different sentences when the sentences could actually be combined:

Wrong: He achieved a considerable degree of success. This success was attributable to hard work.
 Right: His success was attributable to hard work.
 Right: He was successful because he worked hard.

Exercise
Eliminate extra words that add nothing to your meaning.

1. Her mistake was evident to the eye.
2. I personally don't agree with that proposition.
3. The folders are red in color.
4. His views were shallow in depth.

5. The average annual income in our community is $18,000 a year.
6. We have changed many things, such as design, color, etc.
7. He is equally as bright as you.
8. The report was long in length.
9. This floor is restricted just to our personnel.
10. Refer back to Table A.
11. He handled approximately 14 to 18 letters each day.
12. The room was six feet wide and eight feet long.
13. Rewrite the report again before handing it in.
14. Her solution is more preferable to yours.
15. The month of December proved more rewarding than expected.
16. You'll find the answer on page four (4) of the manual.

Possible corrections

1. Her mistake was evident.
2. I don't agree with that proposition.
3. The folders are red.
4. His views were shallow.
5. The average annual income in our community is $18,000.
6. We have changed many things, such as design and color.
7. He is as bright as you.
8. The report was long.
9. This floor is restricted to our personnel.
10. Refer to Table A.
11. He handled 14 to 18 letters each day.
12. The room was six by eight feet.
13. Rewrite the report before handing it in.
14. Her solution is preferable to yours.
15. December proved more rewarding than expected.
16. You'll find the answer on page 4 of the manual.

When you find yourself repeating ~~the same~~ words in consecutive statements, you can often restructure the series into a list.

Original

Demo kits and booths previously used at various shows will be *on display* in the factory. The committee has arranged for a police car and a police motorcycle to be *on display* in the parking area. Many of the products *on display* will be equipped with switches and buttons for operation by the children.

Revision

Display Items

1. Demo kits and booths from previous shows will be in the factory.
2. The committee has put a police car and a police motorcycle in the parking area.
3. Many products will have switches and buttons for the children to use.

If you don't have enough material for a list, try cutting down.

Original

The committee will place 40 guides who will be at strategic points throughout the facility. Having the guides at hand to give personal tours is another of our plans. The guides, placed at various locations in our facility, will ensure the well-being of our many guests.

Revision

The committee will place 40 guides at strategic points, both to give tours (on request) and to ensure our guests' well-being.

Phrases

Examine these modifications.

Phrase	*Modification*
for the reason that you haven't	since you haven't
inasmuch as	since

with the exception of	except for
in order to	to
in the event that	if
for the purpose of	to
with accuracy	accurately
in the process of checking	checking
during the course of	during
in the neighborhood of	about
owing to the fact that	since
due to the fact that	since, because of
with regard to	concerning
prior to	before
at the present time	now, currently
subsequent to	after
in the amount of	for

Exercise

Revise this paragraph to remove heavy phrases.

In reference to your letter of May 12, please find enclosed herewith a check in the amount of $72 for your services. In view of the fact that you have not as yet returned our loaner equipment, we would appreciate it if you would do so without further delay. In the event that you cannot do this, please advise us before you leave the country. Inasmuch as you are leaving the country for a period of a year, we will not anticipate hearing from you during the course of that time. However, it is essential that you get into contact with us subsequent to that time.

Possible correction

Here is a check for $72 to cover your services, as specified in your May 12 letter.

Please return our loaner equipment or tell us if you can't before you leave the country. Also, we need to hear from you as soon as you return.

Prepositional Phrases

Prepositions are directive words like these:

in, from, to, under, of, with, for, between

Typical prepositional phrases are:

in the house, to the man, of the board, for you

Many *of* phrases can be replaced by possessives, as in these examples:

Original: The president *of the company* told the officers *of the company* that *without the approval of the board of directors,* no changes could be made.

Revision: The company's president told his officers no changes could be made *without board approval.*

The original has five prepositional phrases; the revised sentence has one.

Exercise
Change or eliminate the prepositional phrases.

1. All of the newspapers with the exception of *The Bugle* are on strike.
2. The emphasis of this course is on the development of basic skills.
3. The head of our club declared that the changes in our constitution are not valid.
4. We evaluated a variety of methods of making the machine.

Possible corrections

1. All newspapers except *The Bugle* are on strike.
2. The course emphasizes developing basic skills.
3. Our club's president declared our constitutional changes invalid.
4. We evaluated various ways to make the machine.

A final word about prepositional phrases: they crop up whenever a writer is muddled. This passage, which aims to promote automation, hides its message well:

> The daily monitoring of cash balances in corporate accounts influences the efficient use of funds. Moreover, the timely reporting of those balances can increase the investment potential and decrease the loss due to discrepancy. Two problems arise in the human handling of balances—time consumption and possibility of error. The enhancement of timeliness and capacity for information can be attained through the automation of functions.

Unnecessary Verb Forms

We weaken our writing by stuffing it with verb and noun combinations that should be styled as verbs, as in these examples:

Don't	*Do*
make decisions	decide
take into consideration	consider
take action	act
make application to	apply
have discussions	discuss
make revisions	revise
come to conclusions	conclude
make declarations	declare
undertake studies	study
achieve improvements	improve
experience problems	have problems
give assistance to	assist
have a preference for	prefer

Verbs carry more energy when in a pure form. This means that variants of *to be* should not replace action verbs.

Weak: The results are in agreement.
Better: The results agree.

Weak: There will be an increase in property taxes.
Better: Property taxes will increase.

It also means you should not qualify statements you can make unequivocally:

Weak: He seems to be acting badly.
Better: He is acting badly.
Weak: Profits appear to be going higher this year.
Better: Profits are increasing this year.

Exercises

Using the principles we've discussed in this chapter, make these sentences more concise.

1. He has an intense dislike for the writing of reports.
2. The new design should achieve an improvement in the yield of the product.
3. She never makes an attempt to improve her skills.
4. It is considered important to express yourself with ease.
5. There are too many mistakes appearing in this catalog.
6. In order to meet the deadline, we worked overtime.
7. In view of the fact that you made an agreement to pay us, I will expect a check in the amount of $50 next week.
8. In the event that you can invent a machine that is totally unique, I will supply funds for development.
9. Due to the increase in the salary of the employees of the company, the workers who were considering leaving made a joint decision to stay.

Possible corrections

1. He hates to write reports.
2. The new design should improve the product's yield.
3. She never tries to improve her skills.
4. Expressing yourself easily is considered important.
5. This catalog has too many mistakes.
6. We worked overtime to meet the deadline.

7. Since you agreed to pay us, I will expect a check for $50 next week.
8. If you can invent a unique machine, I'll supply development funds.
9. Because their salaries were increased, the workers thinking of leaving decided to stay.

Rewrite this paragraph, leaving out all unnecessary words or phrases.

At your request, the attached preliminary and tentative conceptual memorandum is being sent to you as an outline for the concept of the purchase of new general-purpose equipment. It should be pointed out that this memorandum still must be reviewed by counsel, particularly with regard to certain assumptions of tax calculations and methodology. Should you have any interest in this concept, I would propose that we discuss it further. Because of the desirability of the information contained herein, I know that you will treat same with discretion.

Revision

As you asked, here is a memo outlining the purchase of new equipment. Counsel has yet to review it, particularly concerning tax issues. Please keep all information confidential.

If you're interested, let's discuss it next week.

Make this passage more concise.

I am in the process of compiling a procedure manual. This manual will contain all procedures, policies, etc., which are necessary for the day-to-day activities of our organization.

I would appreciate your comments, suggestions, etc., on what the manual should consist of, its form, function, and so on. Write out your suggestions or see me. Your help is appreciated.

Revision

I am compiling a manual of our daily activities. I would appreciate your suggestions.

Thanks for your help.

2

THE WORD MAZE

Reading many communications today is like being lost in a maze. What is the writer trying to say? What does this or that combination of words mean? Regardless of your education level, you can easily lose your way.

All major popular publications (*Reader's Digest, Newsweek, Time,* for example) aim at an audience with about a tenth grade education. Yet readers don't feel they are being talked down to. Even a highly educated person wants clear, simple prose. A business letter or memo isn't a poem. Its only purpose is to carry a message. If it's unclear, it's useless.

Many people feel they must impress their readers and especially their bosses. Or they represent a prestigious company and want to convey that status on paper. The result is confused, foggy language. Too many communications are ignored because they aren't readable or because they threaten the reader. Which of these two messages is more likely to move the reader to pay the bill?

1. Please be advised that it is the intention of the undersigned to discontinue service if you do not remit full payment within the month.
2. We will cut off your service if you don't pay us by the end of the month.

The danger with the first message is that the reader may not even realize it is saying "Pay up or else." People don't read things that confuse them.

Particularly offensive are business writers who are carried

away with their sense of power when putting words on paper. For example:

Closing Remarks

A conservative approach was taken in making the assumptions used and many of the assumptions are related. In most cases if one assumption does not hold true, another assumption will be as untrue, having an offsetting effect.

The assumptions relating to inventory level were made in the absence of a published inventory report. If actual inventory levels do not agree materially with these assumptions, there will be a substantial impact on our short-term debt levels, and correspondingly on our cost of short-term debt.

Believe it or not, this was written by someone with an excellent job. Pity the staff people who must read it!

Corporate Strategy

Our 1980 business year strategy should continue to build on those plans laid in 1979 when we concentrated on an objective to increase our profit after tax to a minimum of 3.66 of sales by 1981 by developing the higher gross profit opportunities and improving all expense areas. 1980 begins a new decade of challenges that will test the management capabilities of all of us. Overall corporate goals will not change during this period. Therefore it will be more difficult for us to plan and achieve profits that will generate the necessary return on our investment. Improved use of assets is absolutely essential if we are to assure corporate growth during this period. Inflation, competition, and softening of the economy are the factors which should concern us in planning a strategy for success.

These long, inflated sentences illustrate what I call the "cheerleading syndrome." One hears in it the strains of "Let's go, team! Let's maximize our potential by actualizing the growth to which we are inherently dedicated!" Heavy on sound, light on meaning. Breaking the passage into its components shows only these simple assertions:

1. In 1980 (as in 1979) we want to increase after-tax profits by a minimum of 3.66 percent of sales.
2. To do this, we need higher gross profit opportunities and improved expense areas.
3. Our management will be challenged.
4. To grow, we need to improve use of our assets.

Seeing it stripped to its bare bones, you realize it is not a strategy at all. No specific recommendations are made. Someone was simply trying to sound good.

Metaphors are also popular among those who want to achieve an elevated effect. Ships are particularly prevalent.

Announcement

Three new hands have joined the Marketing Department Staff. They will be located in Stonehaven. The general scope of their duties will be to help determine what is of value to our present and future customers. They will also assist general management in setting the objectives and formulating the strategies for delivering customer satisfaction.

Each of the three is brand new to the business as a whole. In this respect, we have a unique opportunity to shape their viewpoints to best help us achieve our long-term objectives for growth and prosperity. Although all problems must be addressed, I suggest we refrain from presenting a negative imbalance of viewpoint to the new people.

Fran Davis, Paul Boyer, and John Segovia will be soon visiting your area. Please expose them to all aspects of your business that are practically possible. You have fertile ground in these people. If we plant well, the rewards will be gratifying and helpful to us all.

Here the poetic reference switches from the ship ("Three new *hands*") to the field ("If we *plant* well"). At best, this is a corny way to describe this simple situation:

1. Fran Davis, Paul Boyer, and John Segovia will soon join the Stonehaven Marketing Department to work on customer service.
2. When they visit you, please tell them as much as you can about your work without stressing the negative aspects.
3. Since they are new to our field, we have the chance to offer them our particular philosophy.

This next passage is another maze. If you can work your way through the thought process, you'll understand what the writer is trying to say.

Evaluation of the USDA safety program by FAA has failed to produce conclusive results. Although air operations procedures used by USDA meet or exceed FAA requirements, the number of aircraft accidents is increasing.

Questions: How does an evaluation produce conclusive results? If no results were shown, what does the sentence about "accident increase" mean?

Most of the problems we discussed in the first chapter—repetition, wordiness, long sentences—lead to ambiguity. If we can organize our concepts around a single theme, the reader will sigh with relief: "Oh, that's what you meant!" Deflate your writing. Don't do this:

Pupil weighting systems are in early development. There is little inclination in the states that have them to give up pupil weighting systems though there will be continuing experimentation with changing pupil weightings and with developing more stringent regulations to prevent undue manipulation by local districts. Pupil weighting systems, unlike categorical grant programs, guarantee that all districts will share in state aid based on educational need. As districts identify legitimate educational needs, states will increase their fiscal support commensurately. A key management problem on the part of interested governments, however, will be the estimation of aggregate educational needs among different local districts.

Do this:

> Although still early in development, pupil weighting systems are ongoing state experiments. Some features of this concept are:
> —Varied pupil weightings (experimental).
> —New regulations to limit local-district manipulation.
> —Influence on state aid—unlike categorical grant programs, this one guarantees shares for all districts, based on educational need. The government will have to assess the different district needs.

Each profession seems to have its jargon or buzzwords to set it apart. Just as children have their own cant, these groups separate themselves from others by using "in" expressions. Educators, lawyers, physicians, and government workers are prime offenders in this regard. For example, note this message written by an educator.

> Each student is to be evaluated on the basis of the quality of work that is accomplished in class in light of his/her ability to do the work that is assigned in each individual case. We, as professionals, are well aware that students differ in their ability to grasp and retain instruction. This is true even in classes where students are grouped for one reason or another. Recognizing and providing for individual differences has long been recognized as a prime objective in teaching.

Translation:

> We should evaluate our students' work on the basis of their ability. Each student is an individual, regardless of the imposed grouping. Our teaching must recognize and provide for these individual differences.

Typical of messages written by government workers is this one.

> Regarding section 4567 and ABCD participation in the Federal Information Locator System, also required by sub-

part A, any information ABCD receives is always related to
a specific project proposed by a particular company. It is,
therefore, doubtful that the information ABCD receives
could be found in another agency or that other agencies will
find ABCD's information useful. That is to say, the FILS
can apparently do little more for ABCD than create extra
work. ABCD apparently could derive little or no benefit
from FILS, nor is it likely that other agencies could benefit
from ABCD's participation.

Note the repetition of the agency's initials, as if by saying
"we" the agency loses status. Reading this passage is like
feeling one's way through a dark maze.

A member of the legal profession characteristically says:

If 50% or more of the total combined voting power of all
classes of stock of Richard Moss, or any successor to Richard Moss, entitled to vote for the election of directors shall
not be directly or indirectly owned by Richard Moss and/or
members of his family (such event being hereinafter referred
to as a "Change in Control"), then effective upon such
Change in Control, you shall be entitled to immediately exercise the options granted to you herein in their entirety in
whole or in part at any time or times between the date of
such Change in Control and the earlier of 90 days after termination of your employment or July 5, 1984.

One might expire before being able to decipher this passage. Does the writer charge by the word?

Physicians, who deal with life and death problems, often
resort to euphemisms. One hospital marks "MFC" on charts
of seriously ill patients; the initials stand for "measure for
coffin." Death may be called *mortality* or *fatality* or *termi-
nality.* One might easily become confused between employment's termination (ending) and life's termination (death).
No longer may we simply quit, get fired, or die.

The more we rely on the same tired words and expressions to convey messages, the weaker our language becomes. Some of the offenders are these:

> *interface, expedite, viable, thrust, meaningful, mandate, implement, execute skills, parameters, awesome, matrix, multifaceted, impact, bottom line*

On the other hand, we've taken to inventing our own forms of the language. Sometimes we add a suffix like *ize* or *wise* to give a false sense of energy to our verbs or nouns. Some examples:

> *prioritize, factionalize, strategize, permanentize, compartmentalize, systemize, sizewise, competencewise, economywise, profitwise*

The media don't help in their exaggerated advertising campaigns. So much of what we hear rings of hyperbole: Honey is described as "pure, natural, and unadulterated"; gum is offered in the "single most favorite flavor"; detergent is "totally unique, unlike any other product you've ever used before." A simple word of praise sounds like a putdown when compared with these heavenly claims. We find ourselves in a world of airline stewardesses promising their undying support. Instead of "ABC Airlines assures you that our most important priority is your comfort and we shall take all means at our disposal to . . . ," we have:

> I would like to congratulate you on this achievement and offer my assurance to you that XYZ Data Control will continue to make every effort to support ABC aircraft to ensure the unqualified success of the BAT plane in the coming years.

Why are people always promising to "make every effort"? How does an "unqualified success" differ from an ordinary success? Our communications would be stronger if we left out the banal expressions. For example:

Congratulations on this fine achievement. We look
forward to helping ensure the BAT's future success by working with you and sharing the development problems.

Think about these suggestions.

Don't: gush, use too many adjectives, or add exclamation
points freely
use "girlish" expressions like "that's really great" or
"I had a really terrific time"
use words or expressions you've heard a hundred
times
Do: try to sound sincere, honest, and open
avoid drama and false excitement
be professional at all times

At times our perception of what management expects is
incorrect. We think our supervisors want impressive or
long-winded language (some unfortunately do); most often
they want the message expressed as clearly and simply as
possible. Upper management certainly doesn't have time for
gaseous prose. One cliché makes sense: Time is money.

3

LIST IT

Huge block paragraphs are hard to absorb. Similarly, too many facts presented in sentence form can put the reader to sleep. The facts themselves don't stand out; they are lost in the mass. Using lists and headings to break down ideas is a way to promote visual appeal, clarity, and emphasis.

Read the following passage quickly and see how much you retain.

Meeting Overview

Attended meeting to determine if the two systems are compatible. The XYZ government has changed their requirements for AVM. They now desire to use the AVM system for all local controls to area controls (the subsystem). There are 750 local controls, with expected long-term system expansion to 1,600 units. The major technical problem uncovered is that as a result of the number of units the AVM system cannot update each local control every second. Mark Brown claims this is a must for any interface with the Ricard Traffic Control System. George Jones stated we require four to five seconds minimum and demanded a complete investigation of all technical questions. Also, he favors the AVM approach for system update.

Granted this is technical information, but the ideas blend into one another with no distinction between different subjects. If the writer had listed the findings and made separate headings for problem and solution to the problem, it would have been immediately apparent that none of this makes sense. The more you hide behind massive paragraphs, the easier it is for you to pretend you're making sense.

Now look at this passage and its revision.

Although there are many views regarding the shortage of boxcars, it is generally agreed that the need for new cars will continue. During the past 16 years, there has been a 14% increase in railroad freight from 658 billion to 753 billion ton miles. It can be noted that during this same period, there has been a decrease in plain boxcars of 51%. Retirements have at best matched or exceeded additions during this period. For example, it is known that of those cars still in use, approximately 20,000 cars per year have been removed from service. It should also be noted that the average age of today's fleet is 15.8 compared to the useful life of 30 years. While the average length of the cars being retired is mostly 50 feet in length and, therefore, you have only to replace 5 cars with new cars—the result is the same, there is still demand for new cars.

Revision:

Despite differing opinions about the boxcar shortage, we assume the need for new cars will continue. Some relevant facts:

1. In the past 16 years:
   a. Freight has increased 14% from 658 to 753 billion ton miles.
   b. Plain boxcars have decreased 51%.
   c. Retirements have matched or exceeded additions. For example, about 20,000 cars are replaced each year.
2. The average age for today's fleet is 15.8; the useful life is 30 years.

Again, lack of coherence raises questions. What is the author's position? What does the length have to do with the need for new cars? If cars are 15.8 years old and they can last for 30 years, why is there demand for new cars? Listing forces you to provide a clear relationship between ideas. You can't hide your mistakes.

Here is another example.

Interest income, which will be received semiannually from the U.S. government securities, will be credited to each client's account upon receipt. We have been advised that clients on the cash basis method of accounting for tax purposes are required to report interest income in the year received and to deduct repurchase financing expenses in the year in which such financing expenses are paid. Financing expenses may be paid monthly, annually, or at the time the bonds mature. However, clients should also note that in order to deduct financing expenses, such expenses should be paid in cash before year end. In this regard, clients should also note that due to compounding effects, the date chosen for payment of financing expenses will affect the total amount of financing expenses incurred. We have been advised that capital gain would be reported in the year in which the securities are redeemed or sold.

Revision:

Interest Income
   1. This is credited to client's account when received from U.S. government securities (semiannually).
   2. Those on cash accounting method must report income in year received and deduct repurchase financing expenses in the year they are paid.

Financing Expenses
   1. _____.
   2. _____.

Headings draw the reader's attention to the general category you're discussing. Once you've identified the subject, the facts are clearly related. Be careful when you use lists or headings. You need an introduction to the headings or list to clarify what you're talking about. Because this memo doesn't have an introduction that shows a relationship between ideas, the results are confusing.

Richard Arnold, driver licensing supervisor, called. All new programs have been canceled, including the WOSH.

Gasoline Sales Down

A major cutback ($50,000) was caused by the following:
1. Lack of snow.
2. Tourists are staying away—no skiing.
3. Gasoline sales are way down.

The Division of Motor Vehicle's revenue depends on the gas tax.

In this example, the writer doesn't show what the cancellation of the programs has to do with gasoline sales being down. You must spell out the relationship between ideas, even if you think it's obvious. A lead-in sentence solves the problem, as in this revision:

Richard Arnold, driver licensing supervisor, called. All new programs have been canceled, including the WOSH. The main reasons for this change are these:

Gasoline Sales Down

Program costs are funded by the gas tax, a major revenue source for the Division of Motor Vehicles. Since this year's heavy snows have kept tourists away from the ski slopes, revenues have been poor.

Program Administration Weak
1. Many program directors are duplicating each other's efforts. For example, . . .
2. Administrative costs are 50% over budget. Areas of waste include. . . .

In other words, if you promise to explain why a situation has occurred, be sure you present a clearly developed argument or discussion.

Underlining and bullets should be used sparingly for emphasis. You're no better off if everything is highlighted than if nothing is. A school system listed its objectives for three pages in this format:

Objectives

○ *Improve Student Attendance*—Efforts must continue to emphasize the importance of attendance and promptness.
○ *Expand Education Opportunities*—In an attempt to assist students who don't perform well in an ordinary environment, a variety of programs will be implemented.
○ *Improve Articulation*—We must improve articulation among schools.

The text would have been easier to follow if the writer had alternated use of paragraphs and bulleted lists, drawing together similar objectives into groups. As originally written, the objectives are repetitive, vague, and monotonous. This next passage is contradictory.

The marketing department has reviewed the recent market share and has found that we are rapidly losing share at a fast pace. There has been extensive research as to why this has been happening and we have come up with the following reasons:

1. Customer awareness—We have failed to educate the public as to our unique features.
2. Sales force—We need to develop a more professional sales team.

"Customer awareness" isn't a reason for losing share, nor is the "sales force." In a list, your reasons must match your lead-in. This revision corrects the contradiction and eliminates the excess language of the original:

After reviewing the recent market share reports, our marketing department has found we're rapidly losing share because of:

1. Lack of customer awareness.
2. Poor sales force.

All items in a series or list must be in parallel form. This avoids confusion. The reader must pause when you change forms. Compare these constructions:

Weak: Representatives met to select committee members, review budget problems, and for recommendation of future projects.

Stronger: Representatives met to select committee members, review budget problems, and recommend future projects.

Weak: John is deciding the following factors next Tuesday at our meeting:
1. When we should announce the new merger.
2. How we can raise profits next quarter.
3. The monthly schedule for mailings.

Stronger: John is making these decisions next Tuesday at our meeting:
1. The date for announcing our new merger.
2. The way to raise profits next quarter.
3. The monthly schedule for mailings.

4

PARAGRAPHING

One benefit of writing is the opportunity it provides to organize ideas into units. These units—paragraphs—depend on a topic sentence to state their main subjects and tie related sentences together. Although it usually opens the paragraph, the topic sentence may also be placed in the middle or at the end.

Which sentence in each example states the paragraph's theme?

Letter writing should be done with a purpose. We want our readers to believe something or react in a certain way. So we write to influence them, using what language tools we can find.

Angry words are flying between Peking and Moscow. Both countries are deploying troops along the border. At the last United Nations meeting, a Chinese ambassador snubbed a Russian ambassador. The dispute between Russia and China is still very much alive.

In the first paragraph, the first sentence states the theme; in the second, the last sentence serves the function.

Paragraphs can be organized in many ways. For example:

Sequence

As in most things, the key to effective dictating is planning. First of all, set aside a time of day when interruptions will not bother you. Then, organize your materials before calling in your secretary. Finally, make sure she has enough time after the session to transcribe.

Reasons or Examples

The Kennedy Center is for all of us. It enriches our cultural experience by presenting the finest artists from America and abroad. Also, it offers concerts, plays, and recitals of the highest quality. Accordingly, this center has become one of the world's most active arts institutions.

Contrast

Heart disease is a leading threat to life. Nearly one million Americans die of it each year. Yet you have several ways to launch a counterattack against this threat. One of the best of these is regular and effective exercise.

Listing

When we offer investors scientifically determined recommendations, we promise to deliver these benefits:
- Leadership in the field.
- High equity return.
- Outstanding portfolio management.
- Ease of understanding.

Question and Answer

What do we expect of management? We expect, at the least, competence, concern, and enthusiasm. In a leadership position, one should. . . .

Each of these paragraphs has a topic sentence and a plan. All the ideas relate to a central theme. A single paragraph can be designed fairly easily once you determine its structure. However, organizing a series of paragraphs is more difficult. Look at the original version of this message.

Customer Service Program

In training an employee for the position of Customer Service Representative, we utilize a detailed training program which encompasses every aspect of the job, to ensure that the employee is fully knowledgeable in all areas vital to the position.

This program has been time-tested, ensuring that within the first two days of training, a representative will acquire a general knowledge of all important procedures, duties, and responsibilities requisite to his job.

Attached is the Customer Service Training Program Outline. Listed in the outline are the sixteen areas of concentration into which training time is divided, along with a time-frame breakdown for each area. These areas of concentration are further broken down into specific topics, providing comprehensive training within each area.

When totaled, the time frames equal sixteen hours, or two working days; this has proved to be an adequate initial training period for proper job knowledge. This, along with follow-up training, results in a proficient Customer Service Representative.

By reducing this message to its constituent themes and assigning each theme to a single paragraph, you can leave out much of the verbiage and provide smoother flow, as in this revision.

Paragraph 1: Our detailed program trains potential customer service representatives in all areas related to their jobs.

Paragraph 2: The program covers sixteen main areas for sixteen hours (two working days). Time-frame and specific topic breakdowns are listed on the attached outline.

Paragraph 3: This initial training and the later follow-up result in a proficient customer service representative.

Actually, the memo says little, so why mask a lack of specifics with a mass of words?

Each paragraph should contain three to four sentences. If you find you have too many short or long units, either join like ideas or break down longer ones. Don't leave ideas hanging in space as this letter does.

Since our recent conversation, I have discussed your account with our credit department.

Their position is that since your company is relatively new, they will need a financial statement to determine whether credit can be extended. This type of information is kept confidential. It is for the exclusive use of our credit department.

If you cannot provide the information requested but wish to seek alternatives toward resolving the problem, please correspond with John Brown.

We appreciate your interest in our products, Ms. Smith, and are eager to work with you in establishing credit.

The letter can be reshaped to have fewer, more cohesive paragraphs.

Concerning our recent conversation, our credit department has asked that you send it a financial statement (required for all young companies). All information will, of course, be kept confidential. If you prefer to seek alternatives, please contact John Brown.

We appreciate your interest in our products, Ms. Smith, and we are eager to work with you in establishing credit.

All the information relating to why you're writing belongs in your first paragraph. This orients your reader. If your first two paragraphs contain background information, join them if you can, as in this example.

Original

At the security supervisors' meeting on October 2, 1980, we had Par counselors attend in order to fill us in on the program for alcoholic recovery. These folks will attend the meeting on October 16 as well.

A number of supervisors at the first meeting wanted to know what the twenty questions were, which if answered "yes" to any three questions would indicate that the chances are, the individual has a drinking problem.

This list of twenty questions is used by the ABC hospital as well as Par counselors. It is as shown below:

1. _____
2. _____
. . . .
20. _____

Revision

At the security supervisors' meeting on October 2, 1980, Par counselors (who will also attend our October 16 meeting) discussed the program for alcoholic recovery and mentioned the twenty questions, a "yes" answer to any three of which would indicate a drinking problem. Many of the supervisors asked for further details.

The list, given here, is also used by the ABC hospital.

1. _____
2. _____
. . . .
20. _____

One way to solve the problem of short, choppy paragraphs is to put some of the data into list form. For example, this series of starts and stops would be smoother as a list.

Original

Our divisional manager has just notified us that ABC department intends to promote Margaret Peace. Margaret is a union rep. with 35 years of experience. The promotion would cause a problem in terms of her salary.

Our salary steps provide Margaret with a base salary of $14,000. As a result of the promotion, she would move to a different pay scale and would effectively lose $500 per year.

To encourage Margaret to accept the promotion, we would have to offer her a bonus to make up the difference.

An added factor is the increased profit sharing she would have in her new position.

We have reviewed the ramifications of the situation and have found that this promotion would not cause any inequities. In discussing it with Margaret, her supervisor should stress this fact.

I authorize you, therefore, to arrange this promotion as soon as possible.

Revision

The ABC department's plan to promote Margaret Peace, a union rep. with 35 years of experience, raises these concerns:

1. Margaret currently earns $14,000 a year.
2. She would earn $500 less a year if she's promoted.

In offering her the new position, Margaret's supervisor should stress these benefits:

1. Margaret would receive a yearly bonus to make up any lost income.
2. In her new position, she would be eligible for profit sharing.

Please arrange this promotion as soon as possible.

A long paragraph such as this next example would have to be revised by breaking it into units.

Career Management Overview
Introduction

A professional sales force is the foundation of every successful high-technology marketing organization. It is through the sales force that ongoing customer relations are established and the marketing objectives of the firm realized. In the communications environment of the 1980s, characterized by ever increasing competition and customer sophistication, the quality of the selling function becomes even more important. However, there is a scarcity of highly skilled professional sales and systems people and increasing competition amongst high-technology industries for these resources. The XYZ system must have the comprehensive human resource management system necessary to attract, develop, manage, and retain a highly qualified and motivated professional sales force. An essential component of an integrated system is the career management subsystem which is designed to build the levels and variety of skills required to meet our marketing objectives today and in the future. With a system of self-management, professional career management's emphasis is on establishing meaningful career pathing networks, thereby coordinating sales force movement from entry level through top management.

The revision might look something like this:

Traditionally, a professional sales force has been the foundation of any successful high-technology marketing organization. It establishes and maintains customer relations, an especially important job because of increasing buyer sophistication in the competitive eighties.

Unfortunately, we are now faced with a scarcity of skilled professional sales and systems people and greater competition for these resources. Accordingly, XYZ needs a human management system, including a subsystem for developing skills to meet our needs. As part of this self-management, we can provide career pathing networks to take the sales force from entry level up through top management.

By reorganizing the passage into units, we recognize that we're dealing with two basic ideas. The first paragraph is about the importance of a professional sales force. The second refers to the scarcity of this force and our need to develop one by establishing a system. If we wanted to pare down our writing to a minimum, we might end with this single paragraph.

A professional sales force, traditionally the basis of a successful high-technology marketing organization, brings in customers and keeps them happy. This function is especially important now since we are faced with increasingly sophisticated buyers, a scarcity of skilled sales and systems people, and a greater competition for whatever resources are available. To meet these challenges, we need to establish a human management system, including a subsystem to attract a sales force and then train it from entry to top management levels.

As you separate ideas into their basic components, you may find yourself left with sentences that need to be pulled together. You should use transitional words to connect some of these sentences. The words will direct the confused reader in the way a street sign directs the confused traveler. Don't use such words in all your sentences, or your writing will become cluttered.

Here are some of the linking words you can use:

In the same direction	and next in addition	also moreover furthermore	besides similarly too
To illustrate	for example	for instance	as an illustration
Contrast	but yet meanwhile	on the other hand nevertheless	on the contrary however still
Conclusion	in conclusion consequently	accordingly in other words	therefore as a result
Time	first	then	finally
Emphasis	now truly	most of all	in fact
Concession	of course	naturally	in fact

Note the linking words in this passage.

Opponents of nuclear power have traditionally stressed the danger of explosion or leakage. *But* recently they've emphasized the problems of storage and waste disposal *in addition*. While governments plan to bury waste in rock formations, opponents of nuclear power question the safety of this solution. Despite recent successes, the antinuclear movement seems to be losing steam.

Now supply the missing transitions in this passage:

It's been two months since we last sent you a bill.
_____(1)_____, you may have sent us the $250 you owe us, and if this is so, please accept our thanks.
_____(2)_____, if you haven't yet paid, please do so within the next few days.
1. Of course
2. However

This next memo and its revision show the effect of drawing together ideas with transitional words.

Original

TI-A should be shut down within the next few months for repairs.

This tower is operating inefficiently. Steam use, solvent loss, and product contamination are all too high.

Reduction in steam is estimated at 8,000 lbs./hr. Steam is $3.60/1,000 lbs. This saving is enough to pay for maintenance of a shutdown.

Safety is a factor. Leaks in lines have been patched temporarily now. Three valves have broken liners.

Shutting down now would allow us to be back in stream for summer production's high rates.

Let's meet tomorrow to work out a schedule.

Revision

For several reasons, we should shut down TI-A within the next few weeks for repairs. First, the tower is not operating efficiently. For example, steam use, solvent loss, and product contamination are all too high. Second, shutting the facility down would result in a steam reduction sufficient to pay for the closing (steam is $3.60/1,000 lbs. and we would save 8,000 lbs./hr.). A third factor is safety. Leaks in lines, temporarily patched, must be repaired and three valves need liner replacement.

Shutting down now would allow us to reopen in time for high summer production rates. Let's meet tomorrow to work out a schedule.

Another way to improve one's writing is to substitute a pronoun for a repeated noun. The procedure is illustrated in these examples.

Poor: The woman, Mrs. Langley, made a fool of herself at the convention. Mrs. Langley stood up and announced that everyone should leave as a protest. Mrs. Langley was surprised when nobody left.

Better: Mrs. Langley made a fool of herself at the convention. She stood up and announced that everyone should leave as a protest. She was surprised when nobody left.

Poor: Everyone knows that some teachers are granted tenure simply because the teachers have worked for a given time. The teachers are then assured of work in our schools, regardless of the teachers' skills or abilities.

Better: Everyone knows that some teachers are granted tenure simply because they have worked for a given time. They are then assured of work in our schools, regardless of their skills.

We'll come back to paragraphing when we discuss different formats. Meanwhile, find which sentence in this next paragraph doesn't fit.

Fear can prevent people from assuming authority. They may be afraid of making the wrong decision and so hesitate to act. Or they may fear admitting they're unable to carry out the boss's orders. Sometimes, superiors may have trouble deciding how much authority to delegate.

Did you choose the last sentence? It clearly doesn't fit with the preceding sentences.

5

EMPHASIS

When you were younger, you may have written like this:

The girl was alone in the house, and she became nervous, and she heard a noise outside. She called out to see if anyone was there, but no one answered, so she tried to forget about it, but she couldn't, and then she turned around and saw. . . .

Children often write in monotonous patterns, stringing together independent clauses. This can put the reader to sleep. It also eliminates emphasis on individual ideas since independent clauses all carry the same weight in a sentence.

To improve your use of emphasis, refresh your memory of how a sentence works. A sentence may consist of:

Phrases: words acting as a unit—they don't have both a subject and a predicate.

Independent clauses: word units with both a subject and a predicate—they could stand alone as sentences.

Dependent clauses: word units with both a subject and a predicate—they begin with a word that keeps them from standing alone as a sentence (*when, since, after, if, although,* and *while* are such words).

Examples

1. *When I rush to the office* [dependent clause], I usually forget something.

41

2. *Running to the office* [phrase], I dropped my papers.
3. Every day before breakfast, *I jog around our block* [independent clause].

Independent clauses within a sentence have equal emphasis, as in this example.

We loved your presentation, but we are sorry we can't use it.

The same point is true here.

We loved your presentation; however, we are sorry we can't use it.

On the other hand, when you use a phrase or dependent clause in a sentence containing an independent clause, something interesting happens. The independent clause is more emphatic than either of the other two, as in these examples:

Although we loved your presentation, we can't use it. [dependent clause followed by independent clause]

Despite the fine quality of your presentation, we can't use it. [phrase followed by independent clause]

In each of these examples, more weight is given to the second, negative idea than to the first idea.

Suppose you're writing to a hotel about a problem you had there recently. You want to say something positive about the good service you've received in the past, but you want mainly to emphasize your current anger. Which of these statements expresses your feelings more effectively?

1. I have had excellent service from you in the past, but I now have a complaint about a recent unpleasant experience.
2. Although I've had excellent service from you in the past, I must protest a recent experience.

Example 2 stresses the negative more effectively and is therefore preferable.

When joining independent clauses, be careful in choosing the connector. Don't use the word "and" to join ideas if they show contrast or a different line of thought. Note these examples.

> Weak: We loved your presentation, and we are sorry we can't use it.
> Weak: Thank you for writing to us, and we look forward to working with you.
> Weak: We didn't complete the project on time, and the client has decided to give us an extension.

As mentioned, one way to provide emphasis is to use a combination of phrases, dependent clauses, and independent clauses. Another way is to subordinate less important ideas by putting them into parentheses or between commas, as in these examples.

> The story (one I heard many times as a child) was dull.
> The painting (one of his lesser works) was just stolen.
> George Brown, a star player on our team, just scored.
> You have to wear proper equipment (goggles) to enter.

Parentheses are used for ideas that are stuck in as a kind of aside. Phrases enclosed by commas carry a little more weight, but they are still secondary to the independent clause.

Dashes highlight ideas, as in these examples.

> Today we're concerned with inflation—a major problem.
> Susan Gold—our favorite babysitter—just graduated.

In each of these next sets of examples, the second sentence offers more emphasis and makes the writing smoother.

> 1. The book contains a complete listing of doctors in your area. It is also a medical reference manual.

2. The book, besides containing a complete listing of doctors in your area, is also a medical reference manual.
1. Margaret Franklin is a geneticist. She lives near me.
2. Margaret Franklin, a geneticist, lives near me.
1. The car comes in silver or dark blue, and it sells for $7,000.
2. The car, available in silver or dark blue, sells for $7,000.
1. Realto is a real estate brokerage system which is leading the industry in terms of restructuring and modernization.
2. Realto, a real estate brokerage system, leads in modernizing the industry.
1. This list is provided by the General Products Committee and is supposed to be updated every six months. This list was compiled from their report dated December 1980.
2. This list, compiled from the General Products Committee's report (December 1980), should be updated every six months.

Exercise

Improve these sentences by placing the emphasis where you think it belongs.

1. Susan Jefferson has only two years of experience. She is the youngest department head we have had.
2. The microprocessor is a complete diagnostic system. It's now reaching the test stage.
3. The jet engine can consist of as many as 30,000 parts. It's an intricate system.
4. He was not a good worker, and he was asked to leave the company.
5. The cell, which was 10 by 12 feet, was quite small.
6. The flowers you sent were wilted, and I don't plan to pay for them.

Possible corrections

1. Susan Jefferson, with only two years of experience, is the youngest department head we've had.

2. The microprocessor, a complete diagnostic system, is reaching the test stage.
3. A jet engine, consisting of as many as 30,000 parts, is an intricate system.
4. Since he wasn't a good worker, he was asked to leave the company.
5. The cell—10 by 12 feet—was quite small.
6. Because the flowers you sent were wilted, I don't plan to pay for them.

Note: You can change the emphasis by turning the sentence around. For example, if sentence 3 were to read "A jet engine, an intricate system, can consist of as many as 30,000 parts," the emphasis would be on the number of parts rather than on the intricacy of the system.

6

TONE

Imagine this as a conversation:

>You: It is suggested, Sam, that you utilize your personnel in a more effective manner.
>
>Sam: I very much appreciate your assistance in outlining the problems encountered in effecting sound business procedures. In order to facilitate the innovations that were recommended by you, I feel certain I should commence by informing my staff herewith as to your recommended changes.
>
>You: Please do not hesitate to inform me if I can be of any further assistance.

Of course you wouldn't speak in so stilted a way—or would you? Recently I've been hearing the pompous tones of business writing in ordinary conversation. Instead of saying "We should begin before the next deadline," people say "We should commence prior to the next deadline." This way of writing or speaking can make others feel inferior. Words carry hidden messages. Whether you plan it or not, your tone will make you sound friendly, angry, sarcastic, pompous, annoyed, happy, or objective.

Business writing should be friendly or, at worst, objective. As a representative of an organization, you should communicate facts, not emotions. Here are some suggestions to keep your tone friendly and positive.

>Use personal pronouns freely and contractions when appropriate.
>
>Use active, not passive, verb forms.

Eliminate archaic and pompous words and phrases from
your writing.
Try to end on a positive note.

Let's see how these points apply to your writing.

Use Personal Pronouns Freely and Contractions When Appropriate

Compare these versions of the same letter:

Example 1

Dear IRA Depositor:

The Revenue Act of 1978 has necessitated the revision of
documents in regard to your Individual Retirement Account. Therefore, enclosed for your careful attention is a
new Disclosure Statement describing the general features of
an IRA and the features we in particular can offer you. It is
advised that the reader pay careful attention to the Disclosure Statement.

We would appreciate it if you would review these documents carefully. In the event that consent is not given to the
amendments made to form 5201, you are required to inform
the undersigned in writing within 30 days of receipt of this
mailing. Otherwise you will be considered to have accepted
this agreement.

Sincerely yours,

The Pension Department

Example 2

Dear Rockland IRA Depositor:

We'd like to draw your attention to some changes in your
Individual Retirement Account resulting from the 1978 Revenue Act.

The enclosed Disclosure Statement describes the general

nature of an IRA and tells you some of the features we in particular can offer you. We think you'll find it informative.

If you don't consent to the amendments, please tell us in writing within 30 days; otherwise, we'll assume you accept the agreement.

Sincerely yours,

John Davis
Pension Officer

Example 2 is friendlier and more appealing because:

1. The direct appeal in the first sentence ("we'd like to draw *your* attention") involves the reader more effectively than the emphasis on the Revenue Act that begins Example A.
2. Contractions (we'd, you'll, don't) make the second letter sound more conversational, less stilted.
3. The language is more familiar and easier to understand.
4. It's signed by an individual, not a department.
5. It doesn't condescend by asking the reader more than once to carefully review.

Use Active, Not Passive, Verb Forms

Active: Subject does the action.
Example: The man ordered a new suit.
Passive: Action is done to the subject.
Example: The suit was ordered by the man.

Passive constructions make your writing sound unfriendly. They also make your writing weak. Sentences have more strength when direct action is involved. It's also nice to know who is doing the action rather than leaving it a mystery.

Exercise

Make these sentences warmer in tone by changing the passive verbs to the active form.

1. On July 6, information was requested by you about the minimum size of our orders.
2. It was announced by our president that refunds will be given to all customers complaining about faulty merchandise.
3. Please be advised that you are requested to contact this office as soon as possible.
4. It is expected that you will be billed on your next statement.
5. Your assistance would be appreciated by us.

Revision

1. On July 6, you asked about the minimum size of our orders.
2. Our president announced we'll give refunds to all customers who complain about faulty merchandise.
3. Please contact this office as soon as possible.
4. We will bill you on your next statement.
5. We would appreciate your help.

In the next example, the many passive forms (italicized) make the writing weak and vague:

A report *was sent* to all departments by the president, who *had been asked* to make comments on the new job safety program. It *was stated* in the report that fewer accidents *were suffered* last year by employees than ever before. Furthermore, the new safety inspector *was named.* All incidents of injury *were to be reported* by him to the president. The report *was received* enthusiastically by the employees.

When you revise this passage to eliminate the passive forms, you find that little is actually said.

The president, asked to comment on the new job safety program, sent a departmental report noting these points:
1. Employees had fewer accidents last year than ever before.

2. A new safety inspector would report all injuries to the president.
Employees received the report enthusiastically.

We now see the confusion hidden by the passive forms. How many fewer accidents were there, what would the president do when he learned of the injuries, and how does the writer know the employees were enthusiastic?

Eliminate Archaic and Pompous Words and Phrases from Your Writing

Pompous	Conversational
the above-mentioned letter	this letter
acquire more information	get more information
please advise me	please tell me
propose alternatives	suggest alternatives
anticipate an increase	expect an increase
in approximately two years	in about two years
let me know if I can be of assistance	let me know if I can help
we should commence	we should begin
if you desire	if you want
you have demonstrated	you have shown
we have employed many methods	we have used many methods
please endeavor to	please try to
we're going to initiate	we're going to start
this should provide you with	this should give you
pursuant to your request	as you asked
per your request	as you asked
please enclose your remittance	please enclose your payment
if I can render	if I can give
if you require	if you need

please allow sufficient time	please allow enough time
if you utilize	if you use

Using the words on the left is not wrong. But the tendency to stuff your writing with them makes you sound formal and stiff.

Try to End on a Positive Note

A glass can be half full or half empty. Similarly, you can say the same thing in different ways.

Negative: If you don't send your payment within two weeks, we'll take legal action.

Positive: If you send your payment within two weeks, you'll avoid the legal action we'll otherwise take.

Negative: Again, we're sorry for any inconvenience we may have caused.

Positive: Again, thank you for telling us about this situation.

Readers remember first the thing they read last, so if you end on a negative note, you'll leave a negative impression. Even in collection letters, you don't want to leave the reader feeling despondent.

The next thing readers remember is the first thing they read. For this reason, you should begin on a positive note. If you apologize, do so in the middle of your letter. Instead of opening with "We're sorry . . . ," you might say "We appreciate your letting us know. . . ."

Being positive means avoiding phrases that annoy your reader. Saying "you claim that" or "you are wrong in thinking" makes your reader uncomfortable. Proving the reader is wrong gains you little. People are more likely to think you're making things up than to believe they are mistaken, regardless of how compelling your arguments are.

TRANSACTIONAL ANALYSIS AND TONE

To understand how to choose words that will best convey your meaning, you need to know something about behavior. Transactional Analysis (TA) theorizes that we act from any of three behavior states: child, parent, and adult. We run into problems when we give unexpected responses. For example:

Situation 1: Your boss asks you to help out in a crisis by working late. His tone is adult and his manner is pleasant. Equally adult, you explain you'd like to help but you have theater tickets. You have given an adult response to an adult request.

Situation 2: Suppose, on the other hand, that your boss says, "You don't understand. I said I need you to work late, and you're on my payroll. You'll work late." He is now adopting a parental tone: Do it or else.

Situation 3: Finally, you're the child when you respond, "Why are you always picking on me? Why don't you ask Linda, who does nothing but file her nails all day?"

In writing, you're childlike when you whine or become excessively emotional, and parental when you talk down to your audience. Which behavioral state does this letter exemplify?

Dear Ms. Brown:

We do understand and appreciate your concern about the possibility of receiving unordered merchandise. However, our records show that last year you accepted our free offer for the 1978 coin collection and paid $17.00 to cover postage, handling, and acquisition. The order form you signed indicated you wished to preview subsequent editions of the coin collection.

In September we wrote to you and all the other subscribers who accepted our offer for the 1978 edition announcing that the new 1979 edition would be in production shortly and would be shipped to you. The letter informed you that you would be billed later. The announcement provided a postage-paid card to be returned in the event you decided to cancel your agreement to receive the collection. When we did not hear from you, we were obliged to send you the collection, and apparently this was not your wish. It is not Hecht's policy to ship unordered merchandise to any customer. In order to get your money back, please follow the directions printed below.

The hidden message is saying, "We were right and you were wrong. However, since we're merciful, we'll grant your request—as long as we can humble you first." The reader feels like a child who has just been scolded by a parent.

The tone of this revision is more adult.

Dear Ms. Brown:

We appreciate your concern in receiving what seems to be unordered merchandise. We hope these facts will clear things up:

1. When you ordered your 1978 coin collection, you expressed a wish to preview later editions.
2. We notified you of the 1979 edition, enclosing a card to be returned if you didn't want it. We didn't get the card back, so we assumed you wanted the collection.

Now that we know your wishes, we'll be happy to give you full refund on your charge account. Just follow the printed directions below to return the collection.

Again, using personal pronouns and contractions can make you sound friendly and gracious. Sounding stiff and formal, on the other hand, creates distance between you and your reader. Since most people resent feeling insignificant in confrontations with big business, you'll be more successful in communicating with the public if you use simple, conversational language.

> Distant: The above-mentioned error has been rectified, and the correction is enclosed herewith.
> Friendly: You were right about this error, and we've enclosed an amended copy.
> Distant: An investigation has been made, and a report will be sent to you shortly.
> Friendly: We've investigated your problem and you'll receive a report soon.

In trying to sound friendly, be careful not to sound non-professional. Contractions are more appropriate for a letter to a customer or an acquaintance than for a formal memo. Slang, clichés, and colloquial expressions such as these should always be avoided in business writing.

> You're terrific! Your work is super, and you deserve a big vote of confidence.
> If we're to nip the problem in the bud, we must seize the initiative.
> I was really thrilled to learn of your promotion!

STROKING YOUR READER

A man opened a bank account and was promised an umbrella as a gift. When his gift didn't arrive, he called the bank and nastily demanded an explanation. The bank representative hung up on him. He called again the next week, this time using a warm and friendly tone, and was soon sent his umbrella. He then called a few hundred banks, claiming to have opened an account and asking where the gift was. Lo and behold, he was so pleasant they believed him! He owned more goodies than he knew what to do with.

Stroking, or making someone feel good, reaps rewards. Which of these expressions stroke the reader?

We're happy to tell you. . . .
Concerning you letter of March 4, . . .
You're right.
I understand how you must have felt.

All but the second are stroking expressions.

Now compare these two versions of a letter responding to a complaint.

Example 1

We note the brochures you asked for were inadvertently sent by regular mail rather than by special delivery. Accordingly, as you noted in your telephone conversation yesterday, they came too late for use.

We regret any inconvenience this has caused you and we are taking precautions to keep this from happening again. If we can be of further assistance, do not hesitate to let us know.

Example 2

You're right. We didn't send your brochures by special delivery, and they came to you too late for use. Obviously, we have caused you difficulty, for which we're sorry. There simply is no excuse for you to have received anything but reliable, excellent service.

Our sales manager, Paul Sorenson, will call you this week to discuss how we will guarantee you fine future treatment. In the meantime, we appreciate your patience.

The important thing in dealing with problem situations is to be sincere in your tone. Show concern. This means expressing yourself as in example 2 rather than throwing tired phrases at your reader. The concept is discussed in greater detail in the chapter on letters.

In general, adapt your tone to the situation and to the pattern already established in the letter you're replying to. Suppose you received this letter.

Gentlemen:
    I'm writing to you to request a new health services book. I put my book somewhere and now can't find it. I'm 84 years old and in good health and I don't expect any problems. But I would like a new book as soon as you can send it. Address it to me, not my husband, so I don't have to tell him I lost it.

Would you begin a response to this lady like this?

Dear Madam:
    Please be advised that we have received your communication concerning your health services book. We shall forward your new book to you within the next few weeks.

Or would you begin more reassuringly? For example, "Of course we'll send you ...," or "We'll be happy to send you. ..." It doesn't take much effort to stroke this woman as in these last sentences.

Exercise
Improve the tone in each of these examples.

1. It is essential that you comply with our request. We shall have to institute legal action against you if you do not remit the full amount of your liability by April 15.
2. Due to an error in processing your order, it will be billed twice to your account. A credit has been issued, and we hope you have not been inconvenienced.
3. We regret to inform you that the merchandise you ordered is not available. Because of this, we have been forced to cancel your order.
4. We were disappointed to learn you aren't taking advantage of our offer of a week's free advertising space. This was a favor we offered at no benefit to us.
5. We note in your letter of August 7 that you claim not to have received your order. We are issuing a second order to be sent without delay.

6. You are mistaken in your assumption that we will pay this bill!
7. This is to inform you that you have been selected to receive a special prize.

Revision

1. If we don't get your check by April 15, we'll be compelled to take legal action. Alternative: If you send us your check by April 15, you'll avoid our taking legal action.
2. You'll note on your next bill that we have mistakenly charged you twice for one order. We've already issued a credit for the duplicate charge.
3. Since our recent offer was so popular, we have run out of coins. Although we must cancel your order, we hope to offer a similar promotion soon and will put your name at the top of our mailing list.
4. Just a reminder about our offer of a week's free advertisement space. We made it available to you to show our appreciation for your continued business and hope you'll change your mind and use it.
5. We are sending you a duplicate blender to replace the one that never arrived (as you stated in your August 7 letter).
6. We will not pay this bill for the following reasons: . . . .
7. We're happy to tell you we have chosen you to receive a special prize.

7

LETTERS

Letters are the most personal of business communications. They can help build relationships, particularly by using a friendly and sincere tone. Formal and stereotyped expressions, on the other hand, keep the relationship between writer and reader stagnant. Who enjoys reading letters that sound like computer printouts?

These expressions are tired and overused:

If you have any further questions, feel free to call
I would like to take this opportunity
For your convenience we have enclosed a self-addressed
    stamped envelope
Thank you for your attention to this matter
Pursuant to (per) your telephone call
We esteem and value your business
Thanking you kindly in advance
Good luck in your endeavors
Your prompt response would be appreciated
If you need further assistance, do not hesitate to let me
    know
According to our records
Attached (enclosed) please find
Permit me to explain
With regard to your invoice
Our company policy dictates
Under separate cover please find
Please be advised
Kindly advise me as to your plans
Answer in the affirmative
We regret any inconvenience this may have caused
I remain yours truly

We use these expressions to dispel writer's panic. If you can't think of anything to say, why not grab for the nearest cliché? Some of these can be easily changed so that they sound a little more relaxed and personal. For example:

If you have any other questions, give me a call.

If I can do anything else to help, please let me know.

Other pat expressions should simply be eliminated. "We regret any inconvenience" is equivalent to saying you don't care at all but you think you should make a gesture. "Enclosed please find" sounds as if you've hidden something and you're now asking the reader to search for it. Also, have you ever seen an envelope that addressed itself?

In writing letters, be direct, sincere, and concerned. Pretend you're talking to someone standing before you, or a person who has just come into your home or office. Don't be afraid to be gracious.

THE OPENING

Time and efficiency experts make two claims. First, they say you should limit your letters to a single page. Apparently, people don't like making the effort to turn the page. Second, they say you should answer a letter as soon as you read it. That way you won't read it, think about it, do something else, read it again, and finally answer it.

Behavioral experts say you shouldn't begin your letters with a stiff reference to a preceding letter. If you do refer to that letter, subordinate the reference. For example, "In reference to your letter of April 14" can be changed to any of these openings:

Here's the information you asked for in your April 14 letter.

Your April 14 letter asking about _____ interested me greatly.

You asked about _____ in your April 14 letter. We've been able to _____.

Yes, you may return your _____ for factory inspection, as you requested in your April 14 letter.

You're right. We forgot to credit your account for _____, as you noted in your April 14 letter.

When we got your letter this morning, we immediately _____.

Thank you for your quick action to _____, as you mentioned in your April 14 letter.

The helpful suggestions you offered in your last letter allowed us to reduce our budget by _____.

Your letter asked about _____. I'm happy to tell you _____.

I can understand your concern about _____, as you brought up in your April 14 letter.

Will you answer a simple question about the matter referred to in your April 14 letter?

Did you ever find the _____ you wrote about last June?

Did you ever get the $40.00 check we sent you in May?

We're sending the materials you asked for in your April 14 letter.

Parentheses also help in subordinating references. You may, for example, change this first version to the second.

On April 14, 1980, you wrote to us to tell us that you ordered a plate from our special collection and that you had never received it. We have sent you the plate.

You'll be happy to know we've just sent you the plate you asked about from our special collection (your April 14 letter).

Use parentheses, too, to subordinate a reference to a substitute reply, as in this example.

Original: Your letter of April 14 has been referred to me
           for reply.
Revision: Your April 14 letter (referred to me for reply)
           asked about our credit policies.

Giving an immediate explanation of why you're writing is important. So is bringing the reader into the picture. A dead reference doesn't introduce your message effectively. Also, don't begin with something the reader already knows. For example, don't say, "You wrote to us on July 15 from New Mexico where you were staying during the last convention. At that time you wanted information about our sales record for March." The reader is likely to be yawning before getting through the first sentence. Again, if you must begin with a reference to a letter or telephone conversation, subordinate it and focus on why you're writing.

Your opening orients the reader. Try using a "you" approach rather than a "we" approach up front, addressing yourself to the reader's needs and interests. You may certainly use the "we" pronoun in your beginning, but make sure you don't leave the reader out.

Weak: We notice in our letter of January 2 that we asked
       you to send us a copy of your brochure. We haven't
       received it.
Better: Did you ever send us the brochure we asked for in
        our January 2 letter?

Weak: Dear Parent:
         We are about to embark upon another school
       year and would like to elaborate on some programs
       our professional staff will be offering. We want to
       assure you that our programs center on enriching
       our curriculum to a maximum extent so that the
       learning experience of each child will be fulfilling.
Better: Dear Parent:
         You will be interested to learn of some of the
       things we're planning for your child this year. We

> know you're concerned about the basics—reading
> and writing in particular—and we share this concern
> with you. So our first project is a skill-building cur-
> riculum designed to fit your child's needs.

The original sounds like cheerleading, more concerned with
impressing than with communicating. The revision offers
specifics, telling what will be done for the child.

THE MIDDLE SECTION

After the orientation come the facts. These can be put
into a separate paragraph or (if the letter is short) with the
orientation. Don't give the facts before orienting the reader,
as the weak example does.

Weak: Dear Dr. Reed:
   We are holding a symposium in Atlanta, Georgia,
in Managing Human Resources on July 5–9, 1981.
Topics to be discussed include The Woman Manager, Public Speaking, and Career Development. We
are expecting over 500 participants.
   We would like to invite you to give a one-hour
lecture on Management by Objectives on July 6
(morning), for which we will pay you $200. We in-
vite you to participate in any of the other sessions
you might care to.
   We will discuss the technical arrangements when
you confirm your attendance. Your reply by March
5 would be appreciated.

Better: Dear Dr. Reed:
Subject: Atlanta symposium on Managing Human
         Resources, July 5–9, 1981
   We cordially invite you to speak on Management
by Objectives at our symposium. From what we've
heard about your speaking ability, your one-hour
lecture would be a highlight of the week.

In exchange for your talk, we'll pay you $200. Additionally, you are welcome to join our expected 500 participants in discussing topics such as The Woman Manager, Public Speaking, and Career Development. It promises to be an interesting exchange of ideas.

May we have your confirmation by March 5 so we can make final arrangements?

Dr. Reed may have thrown the original letter away before learning an invitation was included.

THE CLOSING

Your closing stimulates the reader to action by making a request and/or by adding a personal statement. Often the closing is put in a separate paragraph to make it stand out, especially when dates are included. Be sure to put all dates at the end of your letter. If you mention them early, repeat them at the end. Use specific time references. If you don't know the date, make one up instead of saying "soon" or "as soon as you can." Don't say "hoping to hear from you," or you may go on hoping.

Some examples of closings:

As soon as you send us your application, we'll immediately process it.

Again, thank you for telling us about this situation.

Thank you for your patience with this delay.

May we have your reply by April 6?

I need your answer by June 9.

I would appreciate your quick response.

Just write the answers to my questions in the margins of this letter. You can then return it in the envelope provided.

If you need any other help, please let me know.

Please send the materials promptly so we can complete your order.

Please return two copies of the drawing with your comments.
Thanks again for being so prompt in answering my questions.
Since the project must be completed by Christmas, we'll
need your shipment by November 4.

The basic format for letters is opening (orientation), middle (facts), and closing. If you stay within this design, you'll
grasp the reader's attention, deliver your message, and pro-
voke a response. These letters and their revisions illustrate
why design is so important.

Example 1

Your letter of August 3 to Mr. O'Brien has been referred
to me for reply.
Besides the two letters telling you the order was being
processed, you should have received a third letter telling the
reason for the delay in shipment of the auto battery charger.
The emergency light was defective and the supplier is shipping the charger minus the light at a reduced price.
Our records do not show a shipping date. The order will
not reach you before you move. As UPS will be unable to
forward, please advise if you wish to reorder for shipment to
your new address.

Opening (*orientation*): You're explaining why you're writing. The letter has been referred to you. Another letter had
been sent about the delay—it must have been lost.
Middle (*facts*): Delivery of the auto charger is delayed
because of defective light; supplier is shipping at reduced
price.
Closing: You're trying to make shipping arrangements.

Revision

Your August 3 letter, referred to me by Mr. O'Brien,
asked about the delay in shipping the auto charger you or-

dered. We did write to explain this delay; you obviously never received the letter. I'm sorry about the confusion.

Since the emergency light was defective, our supplier is planning to send the charger minus the light at a reduced price. Our concern now is to get the order to you. We can't send it before you move (our records don't show a shipping date), and UPS can't forward it. Do you want me to reorder for shipment to your new address?

As soon as I hear from you, I'll make arrangements to ship. Meanwhile, I appreciate your patience.

The primary purpose of this letter is to expedite delivery—the customer wants the merchandise. Explanations and apologies are secondary to this action. Assure the reader that you're doing everything you can. Tell why you're writing, give the facts, and then focus on action.

Example 2

Thanks for sending us the sample of the material you're using to manufacture fireproof clothing for our plant. Is your production date still set for May? May we have a copy of the test report referred to in your sales brochure?

Marcia Gordon circulated the fabric swatch among our staff. She's received several inquiries dealing with styles and availability. Do you plan to have a distributor in our area?

Will the uniforms be available in all sizes? If you have a price list, please send us one.

Any information you can give will be appreciated.

Revision

Thanks for the fabric sample for the fireproof material. Marcia Gordon has shown it to our staff, and we have these questions for you:
1. Is production still set for May?
2. Will you have a distributor in our area?
3. Will the uniforms be available in all sizes?

Besides answers to these questions, we'd like a copy of the test report your brochure refers to and a price list (if one is available). We appreciate any information you can send.

The original letter rambles. No transition is provided between orientation and facts, and the writer includes questions without a lead-in. The revision separates the ideas into organized units corresponding to our basic letter format.

Example 3

This letter will confirm that you have been canceled from our Vim Vitamin Program. Because of a program malfunction, some of our previous customer cancellation requests were not processed correctly, and a shipment was sent out subsequent to notice of cancellation. If these circumstances apply to you, please return the vitamins according to packaged instructions. We will then issue any necessary credit plus your postage expense.

Please accept our apologies for any inconvenience we may have caused.

We thank you for your participation in our Vim Vitamin Program and look forward to being of service to you in the near future.

This letter seems to cancel someone from a vitamin program while offering a sales pitch for the program at the same time. The purpose of the letter is obscured. If you don't know why you're writing, the reader certainly can't be expected to make the right guess. The revision orients the reader immediately about the purpose of the letter and explains clearly what action should be taken.

Revision

You may have mistakenly received a vitamin shipment after you canceled from our program. If so, please return the vitamins according to the packaged instructions, and we'll credit your account (including postage).

Thank you for your help.

Whatever the situation, decide why you're writing the letter before you begin. Gather your facts, then order them into an opening, a middle, and a closing. This technique should work for you every time.

PROBLEM LETTERS

When you're dealing with a problem, your letter should alert the reader immediately about the problem that exists. Telling a story without putting it into context is wasted effort.

Suppose you have just received an invoice from the Acme Flower Shop. Several weeks ago you ordered flowers for a client's daughter, in the hospital for the first time. The floral arrangement was brown and wilted. In your phone talk with him the manager agreed to send a replacement, which also arrived in poor condition. After another call, a lovely arrangement was finally sent. However, you feel that the florist's poor service and your embarrassment are cause for nonpayment. How would you write this letter?

If you were to tell a chronological story, you would probably include too many details and lose the strength of your argument. Here's a better way to set it up.

> I've had the following problems with your company:
> 1. Some flowers I ordered for a client's daughter (invoice enclosed) arrived brown and wilted.
> 2. A second order, reluctantly sent by the manager, was similarly poor in quality.
>
> Although a lovely arrangement was finally sent, I'm not paying the enclosed invoice. The embarrassment I suffered because of your poor service warrants nonpayment.

You can also use headings to emphasize your categories, as in this letter.

Dear President:
I've had these problems with your company:

Films Not Received
After confirming my November order of several films for later delivery, I found them not available twice (February in Atlanta and March in Houston).

Response by Your Company
When I called to complain, I was told the problem was my fault for ordering films sent to hotels.

Please confirm your policy of shipping films directly to hotels. Also, if possible, I would like some assurance that films I have ordered for specified dates will arrive on time.

DENIAL LETTERS

In turning someone down, you should go more slowly and take more time than in other kinds of letters. Your task is not simply to deliver facts. You must also soothe feelings, and at times this means being a little more flowery. The essential thing is to be sincere.

Situation:

1. A dean of a business college wants to attend a seminar on writing held at your bank. He wants to set up a similar program at his school and wants some pointers.
2. You restrict your seminars to personnel of your own bank. However, you do offer your services outside the bank for a fee.
3. You can recommend a book you used to design your seminar. Called *Effective Ways to Teach Writing,* it was written by Susan Eliot and published by Brandon Press.

In writing the letter, you should try to make the reader feel comfortable, as this example tries to do.

I applaud your efforts to set up a writing skills program at your college. I'd like to help in any way I can.

My seminars, unfortunately, are limited to bank personnel here at Money Bank. However, I do private consulting and would be happy to discuss my fee if you're interested.

You'll be pleased to know that all information needed to set up a program is available in a book I used. Titled *Effective Ways to Teach Writing,* it was written by Susan Eliot and published by Brandon Press.

Whatever option you choose, good luck with your program. Please let me know if you have any specific questions I can answer for you.

The letter contains several stroking expressions:

I applaud
I'd like to help
would be happy
you'll be pleased
good luck

Which of these rejection letters would you rather receive?

Thank you for applying for our position of personnel assistant. Although we have filled this position with another candidate, we will keep your résumé on file. We will contact you should an opening arise.

Good luck with your future endeavors.

After much deliberation, we've offered our personnel position to another candidate. The choice was certainly hard to make, especially since we found you so personable. Experience in compensation and benefits was the deciding factor.

Please contact us again, Barbara, after you've taken the courses you mentioned.

Naturally, you wouldn't tell a candidate to reapply for the position if you weren't interested. Too many promises of "We'll keep your résumé on file" make this a questionable phrase. If you don't want the candidate to try again, say something like this:

Thank you for applying for our personnel position. Although we've filled the position with another candidate, we do appreciate your interest in our company.

If you have a file and plan to place the applicant's résumé in it, call it an active file and tell the applicant how long it will remain there.

Now compare these versions of a "no" letter.

Your interest in our summer school program is gratifying. Unfortunately, however, you can't have a position with us. You need state certification to teach in any of our programs.

Please contact us if you do get certified. We are always looking for qualified teachers in your field.

Your interest in our summer school program is certainly gratifying; we're always looking for qualified teachers. As soon as you have state certification (a requirement for all our programs), we'll be happy to consider you for a position.

The second example is more positive. The first contradicts itself, first giving a definite no, then making it conditional. Here are another two examples of how to say no.

Negative ending:

We are in possession of the receipts you submitted for reimbursement. We refer you to our members' handbook where on page 7 it states that claims must be submitted no later than 20 days after disablement. Based on this information, all claims other than the one dated 10/10/79 from Standard Service are ineligible.

Positive ending:

You recently sent us some claims for repayment. As stated on page 7 of your members' handbook, all claims must be submitted within 20 days of disablement. Accordingly, only your Standard Service claim is eligible.

Sometimes, in denying an application or a request, you may want to be emphatic and harsh rather than friendly and positive. Your aim might be to make a point so irrefutable that the reader won't challenge it or try to change your mind. How final is this letter documenting why the writer won't give the reader another chance?

Original

Thank you for your letter of January 4, 1980, wherein you say you will neither resign your position nor discontinue your efforts on behalf of the company.

I'm afraid I cannot agree to your request that you receive a second probationary period and not be terminated. Information has come to my attention that, failing to receive proper authorization, you have been absent without permission during normal business hours. Specifically, your time sheets indicate unauthorized absences on December 11, 14, and 15 (1980). Unauthorized absences constitute grounds for dismissal and, unfortunately, these grounds must be invoked in your individual case.

I have instructed payroll to issue a final check to you for your services ending 2/20/81.

I wish you the best in your future endeavors.

This letter has several problems.

1. It begins by thanking someone for not resigning—not appropriate.
2. "I'm afraid I cannot" expresses uncertainty—the last thing the writer wants to convey.
3. "Information has come to my attention" is a typically wasted statement.
4. The letter is repetitious and leaden.
5. The ending isn't appropriate.

When you want to be emphatic, write less. The more you say, the weaker your message. This revision illustrates the point.

Revision

    I cannot agree to give you a second probation as you asked. Your unauthorized absences on December 11, 14, and 15 (1980) are cause for dismissal.

    Payroll will issue your final check for services ending 2/20/81.

COMPLAINT LETTERS

    Humor can sometimes elicit a quick response when you want a complaint corrected.

Gentlemen:

    After buying one of your fancy food processors, I created a mountain of delicious goodies for my family. Now I'm at a loss.

    Your machine has had a sudden, unexplained death.

    Please send immediate advice. We're all suffering hunger pangs.

    If you're not one for humor, try presenting the facts objectively, as in this example.

Gentlemen:

    Four times in the last eight months you've sent me a notice of nonpayment. Since I always pay my bills on time, I find this experience upsetting—especially since I've called twice to report the problem.

    What can you do to help me?

ADJUSTMENT LETTERS

    These letters need tact, understanding, and care. A client in the hotel business recently told me the most frequent complaint he heard wasn't about bedbugs or dirty bathtubs. It was about not being taken seriously when complaining. People want you to take their problems seriously. Regretting inconvenience does nothing.

The reader doesn't care why you messed up or what the internal problems of your organization are. The question is: What are you going to do about it? If you can adjust the situation, be specific in defining your action. "We'll take precautions to keep this from happening again" does not inspire confidence.

If you've received a humorous letter, try to answer in kind.

> We're sorry your food processor has had an untimely death. You might check the base for clogging. As noted in the instruction manual, trapped food can cause problems.
>
> If you've cleaned the base but you're still having trouble, send the unit back to us for repair. We wouldn't want you to go hungry too long.

As much as you can, refer to specifics, not just to "your trouble." If you use a word processor, leave space to name the specific problem (but avoid leaving gaps that would tell the reader it's a form letter). This example is specific.

> Thank you for letting us know about the nonpayment notices we've sent you by mistake. I can understand how frustrating this situation has been for you.
>
> We've scheduled an overhaul of all our equipment for June. In the meantime, I've put a special notice on your account to ensure the excellent service you should expect from us.
>
> If you have any other questions or concerns, please call me personally. You can also speak to my assistant, Charles Davis, who will be happy to help you if I'm not around.

Another rule in making adjustments is to avoid wrongly shifting the blame. How often do things really get lost in the post office? It's more likely the mistake was made in your own mailroom, and you won't get sued for admitting it. People respond well to honesty and sincerity.

Which of these examples shows more genuine concern?

It has come to my attention that you did not receive the supplies you requested for your November 21 safety course.

We deeply regret the holdup, but training new staff in the shipping department has kept us from meeting the November 11 date you requested. Therefore, I have sent the materials by truck rather than by UPS, and you should receive your package by November 19.

I regret any inconvenience.

I've just learned you never got the supplies you need for your November 21 safety course. I'm sorry you had to wait and I'll rush the materials to you by truck rather than UPS. You should get them by November 19, in time for preparation before giving the course.

We appreciate your patience with this inexcusable delay.

The first example spends too much time on the writer and the company's problems. The second is more action-oriented, stressing the solution rather than the problem or its cause. Also, the second has a more positive ending.

Focus on action is also evident in this letter apologizing for a flight attendant's rudeness to me.

Dear Ms. Brill:

Thank you for your fine words about our airlines and for writing about your recent problem with a flight attendant. You are right—customer service is our highest priority, and we certainly plan to act on what you've told us.

First, we've told Ms. Bernard's supervisor about your letter. Within the next week he'll discuss her lack of courtesy to you with her. Also, your letter will be placed in her file. We do use our files for evaluating and referencing behavior.

Second, we offer our sincere apologies to you and hope you'll continue to think of us as offering fine, courteous service. There's no excuse for what happened.

Again, we appreciate your taking the time to write.

If the airlines had said "ABC airlines strives to give its customers the finest service" or "We'll make sure this will

never happen again," I would have been less than con-
vinced. The first statement sounds like a slogan; the second
is insincere. You should not make promises to your reader
that can't be carried out.

Here's another example of sincerity.

> Dear Mr. Drew:
>
> I'd like to respond to your complaint (referred to us by
> the *Houston News*) about the suitcase you never received.
>
> You are right. We did mix up your order. Since our pro-
> cessing department never got your check, it charged your
> account for the suitcase. It then incorrectly entered the order
> number, and the order was canceled.
>
> Mr. Drew, I can certainly understand your frustration
> with this confusion, and a simple apology won't make up for
> the trouble we've caused you. But we are sincerely sorry and
> wanted you to know this.

You might as well admit fallibility. No one is likely to sue
you for admitting a simple error. More important, your con-
cession will make the customer feel good.

Which of these expressions sound sincere?

> We strive for customer comfort.
> We've spoken to the clerk and this will never happen again.
> You're right—we did lose your check.
> There's no excuse for this to have happened.
> We hope you'll give us another chance.

PROMOTION LETTERS

When you "sell" the advantages of your organization in a
letter, don't use too many adjectives to generate reader enthusiasm. You sound childish if you gush. Instead, try a soft
approach, relying on facts rather than puffery to convey a
positive message. The unneeded intensives in this next letter
are italicized.

Original

Dear Ms. Regan:

Thank you for giving me the opportunity to discuss with you Optec's advertising plans for the fall. You mentioned that GOLDPOWER is one of three magazines you feel *very* strongly about as an advertising medium for your new campaign.

Since its inception in April 1962, GOLDPOWER has grown significantly in circulation and *total* audience, and Optec has been a loyal advertiser during the *entire* time.

Now that we are in the eighties, the *overall* impact is even greater. Inflation is in double digits and people are *very* concerned about their *inflation*-diminished resources. That is why it is so important to use GOLDPOWER to reach the reader who is aware of purchasing a product that represents quality, value, and a *great deal of* class—like Optec sunglasses. The GOLDPOWER reader is willing to pay more for these benefits. For example, our subscription rates are up by 15%.

GOLDPOWER is a magazine that is right for the eighties and is *very* healthy *in every way*. If there was ever a time to advertise in GOLDPOWER, it is now, because we are a *very* unique *vehicle* and *definitely* a timely one for Optec.

Revision

I was pleased to discuss your fall advertising plans with you and to learn you're considering GOLDPOWER for your new campaign. You may find these particulars about our growth and features helpful in making your decision.

Since our 1962 beginning, we've grown significantly in circulation—22% in just the last three years. In the eighties, with inflation in double digits and the public concerned with diminishing resources, our magazine can offer you special advantages. We represent quality and value, benefits readers are willing to pay for. We reach 10 million wearers of sunglasses, a young population concerned with the kind of styling Optec can provide. Additionally, a recent poll of readers showed our subscribers trust the products they see promoted in our pages.

This is the right time—the best time—for you to invest in GOLDPOWER.

PRAISE AND EVALUATION LETTERS

As with promoting a product, the more you say in praising a person, the less impact the message will have. Do you agree that the revision is more subdued and sounds more sincere than the original?

Original

Last week Alan Christopher and I had the distinct pleasure of working with Lt. Colonel Gary Fay in our automobile safety course.

His cooperation, expertise, and professionalism were outstanding. The class benefited from his keen insight and understanding. Gary's interaction and leadership added greatly to making the program a rewarding experience for all involved.

Gary's example shows that proper education and training can help make safety a significant concern for our Armed Services.

Once again, we appreciate Lt. Colonel Fay's participation. Under his guidance, we know your future safety programs will be of enormous benefit.

Revision

Last week Alan Christopher and I enjoyed working with Lt. Colonel Gary Fay in our automobile safety course. His insight, cooperation, and leadership helped make this a rewarding week for the participants.

Through Gary's example, we see how driver safety can become a significant concern for the Armed Services. Good luck in all your future programs.

Americans love descriptive adjectives. I remember seeing a menu offering fresh-frozen (as opposed to stale-frozen?) orange juice. We tell people they have keen insight—do we think about what we mean before we utter phrases we've heard thousands of times?

Which of these thank-you notes shows more concern?

Thank you for showing us around your factory last week. We were most impressed with everything we saw and feel you should be proud of your fine achievement. We also appreciate the fine dinner and all the other nice things you did for us during our stay with you. You're an excellent host.

Bob and I thank you for your many kindnesses last week. The trip through your factory was special—I had no idea you had developed machines that can put out a new widget every 14 seconds. As for the dinner, where else can you find pheasant and lasagna on the same menu with everything tasting fresh and delicious? Lastly, your picking us up at the airport as a surprise was typical of the special treatment I've come to expect from you. In short, you're an outstanding host, and we appreciate all your care.

The more specific you are, the more convincing you will be. Overuse of compliments is not effective, either for thanking or for evaluating.

PERSUASION LETTERS

Once in a while you may feel you must win someone to your point of view. If your reader is unlikely to be persuaded by facts, you may have to use persuasion. Examine this situation.

1. Mark Walters, branch manager for your company's Florida office, wants you to hold the next diamond merchant's meeting at his home base. He claims his only reason is that the security is better there than in New York,

where you are located. You suspect he simply doesn't feel like coming to New York.

2. If you hold the meeting in New York, you'll save money: four of your staff would have to fly to Florida, and only Mark would have to come to New York.
3. Mark is right—the security is superior in Florida. However, New York's security is adequate, and you've never had a problem.

What should your approach be? Do you hit Mark over the head with your financial argument? After all, you are right. You can appeal either to his sense of fairness or to his self-interest. You can try a technique of negotiation, conceding points. Evaluate these two versions of the letter to Mark.

Dear Mark:

I feel strongly that you should come to New York for the Diamond meeting. Here are my reasons:

1. It would cost more to send four of my staff to Florida than for just you to come to New York.
2. New York's security is not as good as Florida's, but it is adequate.

I'm sure you see the justice of this argument. Please plan to be in New York on December 4.

Dear Mark:

Florida certainly has great appeal at this time of year, and you're right, of course—your security system is superior. On the other hand, have you thought about these alternative benefits?

Given the current economy, the cost saving of bringing one person (you) to New York as opposed to sending four of my staff to Florida would be great—at least $2,000 in travel and expenses. Also, our security is certainly adequate; we've never had even a small problem.

To top it off, we're looking forward to taking you to Martell's, one of the Big Apple's best restaurants, and to getting you tickets to any show you'd care to see. We'll even pick up your hotel tab if you like.

Mark, let's think about holding next year's meeting in your inviting sunshine. For now, I hope I can count on seeing you in New York on December 4.

The second example entices Mark to New York by offering him tangible rewards. In presenting its cost-saving argument, it specifies a dollar amount (your argument is stronger when you talk in specifics). The tone is less threatening, friendlier. In short, the second example is more likely to receive a positive reception. The first might easily be thrown away in anger.

COLLECTION LETTERS

Many companies devote effort and resources to making sales. Yet when the time comes to collect, they suddenly change into cold, impersonal machines. Why not try being personal and warm when asking for your payment? Appeal to the reader's sense of fairness. You're concerned about the welfare of your customers, not just about their money. You might try one of these six approaches.

One reason we don't like to see a high outstanding balance on your account is that it may induce you to stop ordering our fabric. If you owe us money, you'll probably be hesitant to continue dealing with us. In that case, you'll lose a fine product and we'll lose a special customer.

We'll both benefit from your sending $380 to cover our last two bills. And while you're at it, why not order some new supplies at the same time?

Do you have some reason for not paying your $500 bill? If we can help in any way, please tell us. For example, you may prefer to pay in a few installments or defer all payment for another month.

As long as we know you do plan to pay, we can arrange something. Please call me collect during the next week or send your $500 payment. Either way, you'll avoid the unpleasant action we'll otherwise have to take.

We've sent you many reminders about the $82 still outstanding on your account. Surely your credit rating with us is more important to you than this amount.

Why not send us the payment today? You'll feel more comfortable, and we'll be happy to hear from you.

Have we forgotten something? Is it because we've let you down in some way that you haven't sent your $90 check? If so, let us know. We'll be happy to correct the problem.

If, on the other hand, you're satisfied with our care and service, won't you complete your end of our bargain?

The word "delinquent" evokes a harsh image. "Paid in full" is much more pleasant. Won't you let us change the status of your account so that we can list you again with our best customers?

Just use the envelope provided to send us your $50 check—and mail it today, please.

Have you been thinking of paying us the $70 you owe us but not found the time?

Why not relieve your mind and ours by sending us your check today?

FORM LETTERS

Being personal is essential for form letters, even when you send them to thousands of people. Here are some ways to make your readers feel as if you're directing an individualized message especially to them rather than an impersonal, general form letter.

1. Don't set your word processor so that gaps will appear, either where personal items are typed in or at the bottom of the page for a short message.
2. Use personal pronouns (I, we, you) freely.
3. Use contractions freely.
4. Be as specific as possible.
5. Avoid stereotyped expressions.
6. Ask direct questions.

Which of these two examples is more personal?

> Because of an error in processing your order for the star-shaped ring, it will be billed to your account twice.
>
> A credit has been issued to remove the duplicate charge from your account. It is hoped this explanation will allay your annoyance when you review your bill.
>
> If you have any further questions, please feel free to call.

> When we processed your order for our star-shaped ring, we mistakenly doubled-billed you. However, on your next statement you should see the credit we've already issued to correct the error.
>
> I hope this explanation clears up any confusion we may have caused in your billing. Otherwise, if you have any questions at all, please call me collect.

GENERAL POINTS FOR LETTERS

1. Never send out an angry letter. Put it aside until you're sure of the right tone to use.
2. Be sincere. Don't make claims you and your reader know are false. For example, it's foolish to claim you'll fire a clerk for poor service.
3. Say thank you and express satisfaction freely.
4. Anticipate and answer questions before they are asked. Dates and places are particularly important.
5. Admit you're wrong when you can.

6. Be reader-centered. Be sure your communications are clear and easy to follow.

SAMPLE LETTERS
FOR DIFFERENT OCCASIONS

Your promotion to sales manager of the ABC department was good news to all of us. Obviously, your excellent record—six new accounts for just last month—was noticed.

We're really pleased for you and look forward to working with you in the coming months.

My eight years experience as a controller should qualify me for the position you advertised in *The Times* today. The enclosed résumé details my background.

May I have an interview? If you'll call the number given here, I'll be happy to arrange a convenient time.

We were all sorry to hear of your recent loss. Please extend our sympathies to your family.

Just a brief note to congratulate you on your new position in operations control. Obviously, a position so closely related to your educational background will challenge you and benefit the whole company.

Let us know if we can do anything to make your transition easier. Or just stop by when you have a moment. We'd like to welcome you in person.

Thank you for your recent order for a copier. We're pleased to have you as a customer.

The credit information you've sent us, however, is not sufficient. Since further investigation may delay shipment beyond the time you're willing to wait for your new machine, I suggest you send us a check for $780. If time is not crucial, you can send a financial statement to our credit department.

Either way, we look forward to hearing from you soon.

Exercise

Revise this letter so that it sounds less negative.

Dear Ms. Jones:

We cannot comply by making an adjustment related to the claim you submitted on the stereo you purchased from our company.

We want to emphasize that we don't make adjustments on merchandise when the customer has kept it for a week. You claimed the stereo had a faulty sound mechanism, but our final inspection proved it was in excellent condition when you received it.

Because of our policy, we regret to inform you that no adjustment can be made.

Possible revision

Dear Ms. Jones:

We appreciate the concern you recently expressed about your Soundex stereo.

We accept products for refund only if they're returned within a week of purchase. However, we'll be happy to look into your sound problem if you'll send the equipment back to us (address on warranty card). If the problem comes under warranty, we'll repair it without charge. Otherwise we'll charge you for parts and labor, giving you an estimate before we begin.

Exercise

Reorganize the following letter by separating opening (orientation), middle (facts), and closing.

Dear Sam:

Betty and I are still concerned that, after several phone calls and much discussion, you still haven't revised your bill for remodeling our kitchen cabinets. As you know, the two people you suggested we call for a recommendation of your work led us to believe your work was superior. Obviously, the results show clearly that this was not so. We were misled. The door on one cabinet is four inches too wide. This is only the beginning.

The hinges on several of the doors are not attached well. The doors are hard to open and close. You ordered the wrong quantity of formica, to say nothing of the quality, which was poor. Your original estimate was for $1,250. You said you always finish within $100 of your estimate. Since my final bill was for $1,750, I call you a liar.

The two people you suggested we call said you do lovely work in a short period of time. Our kitchen cabinets leave gaps where the doors don't fit, and it took you two weeks longer to finish than you said it would. Another big, fat lie. Besides, we had the added expense of eating out.

Here's a check for $1,250. If you don't like it, that's your problem.

Revision

Dear Sam:

Betty and I have called and written several times, asking you to revise your bill for our kitchen cabinets and correct the problems in workmanship. To summarize our complaints:

Excessive Cost

Since you always stay within $100 of an original estimate (see copy of letter enclosed), the extra $500 beyond the quoted $1,250 is unfair. We shouldn't be charged for the mistake you made in ordering the wrong quantity and quality of formica.

Poor Workmanship

1. Door of one cabinet four inches too wide
2. Hinges on several doors attached improperly
3. Doors hard to open and close
4. Gaps where doors don't fit

Time Taken

The work took two weeks longer than estimated, causing disruption of my family's comfort and the added expense of eating out.

Although the two people who recommended your work gave you high grades, we've obviously been disappointed. When you've corrected all mistakes in workmanship as listed, we will pay you the amount of your original estimate, $1,250.

Please call any evening this week to arrange a date for repair.

8

MEMOS

Like all business communications, memos inform, ask, persuade, or build goodwill. However, unlike letters, memos move within your company or department and rely less on public relations. The key to good memos is organization and visual design. All memos can fit within one of four basic designs. Overall, the format can be summarized as follows:

At top left, tell:
To:
From: [most people initial their name—don't sign your memo]
Subject: [make this as specific as you can within the space allowed]

For the actual written part of your memo, use:
Opening—orients the reader to why you're writing.
Middle—offers facts and figures; possible use of headings or list.
Ending—sums up what's been said, requests action, or adds a personal note.

FORMAT 1—THE TRIANGLE PRINCIPLE

Writers often wonder what to put first, their main argument or the rationalization for that argument. For example, suppose you have this series of items.

1. Last week four secretaries complained of overwork.
2. We've hired two new managers.

3. We have three new accounts.
4. One of our typists just left to have a baby.
5. For these reasons, we should consider adding four people to our support staff.

We could order the items according to a deductive line of reasoning. Deduction follows a line of thought to a "therefore" conclusion, as in this example:

Technell has flourished since its acquisition of a medical technology company last year	→	but it hasn't fully developed the potential of this company in foreign markets	→	therefore, we should study ways to expand the new branch

Arranged in this way, the earlier items would be ordered chronologically, as follows:

Last week four secretaries complained of overwork. Also, we've hired two new managers and we have three new accounts. Finally, one of our typists just left to have a baby. For these reasons, we should consider adding four people to our support staff.

We could also structure the items according to an inductive line of reasoning. Induction makes a statement of inference on the basis of the supporting reasons that follow it, as in this example:

We should expand our new medical technology branch	→	because it hasn't been fully developed	→	despite its favorable impact on the company

When we put the "therefore" conclusion first, something interesting happens. We often find we can leave out the first statement, the historical background. We're then left with the essentials.

We should expand our new medical technology branch because it hasn't been fully developed.

When you give an argument chronologically, you often include irrelevant information. When you put your conclusions first, the reader can evaluate all the information in light of your main point. This next revision illustrates the point.

We need to add four people to our support staff for several reasons. First, last week alone four secretaries complained of overwork. Also, we've hired two new managers and we have three new accounts. Finally, one of our typists just left to have a baby. Why don't you call the agency to arrange for some interviews?

This structure avoids the guessing game that occurs when you put your main point at the end. "Why are you telling me this?" asks the reader who hasn't read the ending.
In general,

1. State your main idea as soon as possible.
2. Follow with a rationale or with supporting details.
3. Avoid historical background unless it's relevant.

Put your rationale first and your main idea later in these circumstances.

1. When your reader is unlikely to agree with you, and you want to make your point before presenting the heart of your argument.
2. When you want to explain something your reader may reject through lack of understanding.

The Triangle Principle for organizing memos relies on inductive reasoning. It's useful whenever you have a point of view or an opinion you want to present persuasively. The point of view is stated at the top of the triangle, followed by a logical progression of specific reasons and examples. This is the format.

1. Point of view or opinion
2. Reasons
3. Examples to support reasons
4. Summary of point of view or action desired

As a working formula, it looks like this:

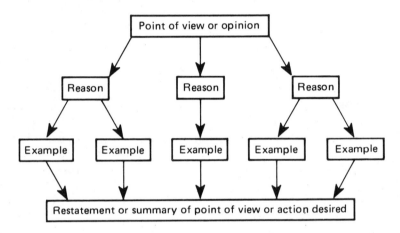

The Triangle Principle is useful whenever you have a point of view you want someone to accept. The more facts you use to support your opinion, the more persuasive the memo will be. This next memo relies more on personal feeling than on facts and is therefore weak.

After a great deal of thought, I've concluded that it's about time we bought respirators for each employee and made it a safety requirement that each employee wear one. I think such an investment would boost morale and cut down on absenteeism and sick leave. Also, employees have warned us about their low morale and the retaliatory measures they'll take through their union if adequate relief isn't offered. If we can correct this situation, it would be good public relations.

The writer's vagueness provokes several questions. For example:

1. How much respiratory-related illness is there?
2. How does the writer know morale in general is low? How many workers have threatened to leave the industry?
3. What has the union threatened?

When you organize according to a plan, you avoid rambling.

When you have many reasons to support your argument, you may want to organize them into two or three general categories. In this case, everything relates to either employee or company benefits. The resulting memo would look like this.

We need to buy respirators and make their use mandatory for all employees for these reasons:

1. *Employee Benefits*
   a. Health—respiratory-related illness has gone up 27% during the past two years.
   b. Morale—a recent survey shows that 12% of the work-

ers are thinking of leaving the industry because of health impairment.

2. *Company Benefits*
   a. Production increase—as absenteeism decreases, our profits will go up 7%.
   b. Avoidance of union action—a strike, threatened for May 3, can be averted if we buy the respirators by April 28.
   c. Public relations—articles in local publications about our attempts to improve health standards will help change the poor image we now have.

Let's get together by March 10 to discuss brands and prices.

FORMAT 2—
PROBLEM-ANALYSIS-SOLUTION

Sometimes we're trying to alert our readers to a problem they should avoid. Yet we hide the problem in verbiage so dense that the reader never finds it. Often, this happens because the ideas are ordered chronologically. We tell a bedtime story, a "once upon a time" tale. This next example illustrates the problem.

Original

At the end of each fiscal month, we are sent a box from each COC containing insurance reports and statistical analyses. The box from Chicago was late in arriving this month. After several phone calls to the Chicago operating center manager, I found out the box was sent to us on November 14, not by the usual way, which is Bankers Dispatch, but by Parcel Post.

I alerted everyone in our company who might come into contact with it to be on the lookout, and I called the warehouse and spoke to Fernando, asking him to check our boxes to see if by chance they were still there. Jan S. phoned me on December 4 and asked me to pick up our box, which she had received from Fernando. The box was sent to the warehouse with the returns, and Fernando has no idea how they got there. In the meantime, the Chicago office fired its mail clerk for not following orders.

I feel that the situation should not be taken lightly and that those who are responsible for receiving returns should be advised about how vital they are so this situation will not occur again.

Mixed in with the excess story telling is a hidden message. We can state it more clearly if we describe the problem, its analysis, and its solution.

Problem: Incorrect shipping of COC boxes
Analysis: Sent by Parcel Post
Solution: Must be sent by Bankers Dispatch

Revision

We've recently had a problem with the incorrect shipping of COC boxes (statistical analyses and insurance reports). Specifically, last month one box was mistakenly sent by Parcel Post and was lost in the warehouse for several weeks.

From now on, be sure to send COC boxes by Bankers Dispatch.

Try putting this memo into a problem–analysis–solution format.

Original

I have indicated to your previously that we appear to have excessive problems with the secretarial and clerical staff. The manifestations of the problem are frequent complaining and high turnover. Inasmuch as this support staff is relatively well paid, the physical environment is pleasant, and the work is not unreasonably burdensome, one might expect to have more contentment.

The secretarial and clerical staff comprises almost one-half of the corporation's population, and attrition is a particular problem because it is extremely difficult to recruit outstanding applicants in these occupational categories. It is therefore imperative that we make every effort to resolve the problems that this group of employees feels are peculiar to them.

In an attempt to determine more accurately what members of the support staff think some of the more serious problems are, we have designed a questionnaire to be sent to all secretarial and clerical employees. Please review it (attached) and give me your comments by c.o.b. on February 2.

Problem: Complaints and turnover among members of support staff.

Analysis: Complaints are surprising; turnover is serious—difficult to recruit good staff.

Solution: Questionnaire.

Possible revision

We're having an ongoing problem with our support staff. Specifically, we're concerned about the frequency of complaints and the high turnover.

The complaints are surprising since work conditions are good (including pay, physical environment, and demands).

The high rate of attrition is a special burden since support staff makes up almost half our population, and outstanding applicants are hard to find.

Please review the questionnaire we're planning to circulate as a survey of support staff attitudes. I would appreciate your comments by February 2.

Here are some other examples:

Original

The instructor survey has identified a problem with distribution of your instructor patches and certificates. Several instructors are not receiving their certification and patches. Effective immediately, all instructor patches and certificates shall be sent directly to the recently certified instructor. We will not send any patches or certificates to the schools. A copy of the class list will be sent to Tom Smith. A supply of patches will be kept by Susan Masters.

Revision

Our instructor survey has uncovered this problem: Instructors completing our courses aren't getting their certificates and patches. To remedy this, please do the following:
1. Send certificates and patches directly to the newly certified instructor, not to the schools.
2. Send Tom Smith a copy of the class list.
3. Give Susan Masters a supply of patches.

Original

The accounting department has recently found that the company policy relative to business meals is not being followed by the employees reporting to you. The company requires each employee to report the business meals on the Expense Report and not to use petty cash vouchers. Also, the company needs to implement all guidelines prescribed in company policy relative to IRS requirements for "Business Meals." Please advise your employees to follow company policy at all times.

For some reason, companies are more eager to talk about company policy than to highlight this policy for their employees. If you say what your problem is clearly and briefly, and do the same for the solution, they will pay attention.

Revision

We're having a problem with incorrect reporting of business meals, as noted by the accounting department. Employees are using petty cash vouchers, not the expense report required by company policy (based on IRS guidelines).

Please ask your employees to use expense reports for all business meals.

FORMAT 3—PROCEDURE

Using this format, you first spell out the procedure, then either explain what will happen if it isn't followed or give an example of what has happened. Visual design is important. Set up your ideas so that they are easy to follow. Two examples illustrating this format are given here.

Original

On your arrival at work, please sign in on your time sheet. Sign out and in during the lunch break and fill in your departure time at the end of the workday. Failure to do so will cause problems concerning your pay. If you do not sign in, you are considered absent for the day. On receiving your time sheets at the beginning of a new time period, please sign your signature. In case of absence your time sheet can be processed.

Revision

Please follow this procedure for signing in and out.
1. Sign in on your arrival at work.
2. Sign out for lunch and sign in on resuming work.
3. Sign out on leaving at day's end.
4. Sign in at the beginning of each time period (so we can process your time sheet when you're absent).

By following this procedure, you will avoid paycheck problems when you're absent.

Original

In order to maintain a record of typewriter and calculator repairs, I have requested that all repair calls be recorded in a Service Repair Call Book. That book will include name of caller, department, and serial number. The books are sequentially numbered. Accounting must also receive a form containing the service number, which is a five-digit number beginning with 18801, and other pertinent information.

This memo has at least two defects.

1. No actual commands are made. When you say "I have requested . . ." you're not actually asking anyone to do anything. Use the command verb form (see revision).
2. Action and excess language are mixed; the reader has a hard time deciding what to do.

Revision

Please follow this procedure in recording typewriter and calculator repairs:
1. Record all calls in a service book, including name of caller, department, and serial number.
2. Send accounting a form noting the five-digit service number (beginning with 18801).

FORMAT 4—INFORMATIONAL MEMOS

When you don't have an opinion to promote, a problem to describe, or a procedure to outline, you simply have information to offer. Your presentation will be clearer and easier to follow if you outline your ideas before you write them down. You'll then be able to identify what I call "process" in writing—the documentation of unnecessary details such as who said what to whom.

Your first task is to ask yourself why you're writing— what the purpose of the memo is. That sounds elementary, but too many people write memos like this:

Subject:Watsbox

The telephone calls for the period June 21 through August 16 have been reviewed. The breakdown is listed on attached sheet A.

The 9-1 calls not logged in wire transfer were legitimate calls, and at this time it is impossible to pinpoint offenders. Bills run after August 17 can be traced through dictaphone equipment; the attached bills run only through August 16.

The C and P detail statements have been reviewed. There was one suspect call, which was investigated and found to be legitimate. Bob R. says it is impossible to dial a speed number and automatically be switched to 9-1. The caller has 17 seconds to break the wrong contact. In the morning meeting of September 26, the violation figures for this number were discussed. All the employees were made aware of disciplinary action. The employees stated adamantly that the Watsbox was being utilized.

Why was this memo written? Certainly not to discuss a problem, for the employees claim nothing is wrong and all suspect calls were found to be legitimate.

After you decide why you're writing and what response you want from your reader, the next step is to outline your ideas as they occur to you. Then, leaving out any irrelevant ideas, reorder them in the sequence: opening (orientation), middle (facts), and closing. By using this formula, we can change the next memo (filled with irrelevancies) into a more efficient product.

Original

Veronica Larson has recently informed me that December 29, 1980, would be her last day of work here as she is moving to California. She inquired about the possibility of a transfer. I was given the name of Stuart Brown, personnel manager at Hillside, whom I contacted and with whom I discussed the matter. At the present time there are no openings in our field, but they do expect a turnover. I made arrangements for Veronica to be interviewed and evaluated by Mr. Brown upon her arrival in California and have given her the necessary information on how to contact Mr. Brown.

I am requesting at this time that a copy of Veronica's

original application be sent to Mr. Brown and that she be given a 30-day relocation leave of absence effective 12/29/80.

Purpose of writing: To ask the reader to take action; to give enough background so that the action makes sense.

Facts:
1. Veronica Larson wants to transfer to Hillside, Calif., on 12/29.
2. S. Brown, Hillside personnel manager, will interview her for future openings.
3. Give her 30-day relocation leave and send Mr. Brown a copy of application.
4. Dec. 29 will be her last day of employment.
5. She inquired about the possibility of transfer.
6. I was given the name of . . . whom I. . . .
7. I made arrangements to . . . and have given her. . . .

When evaluated in light of the purpose, statements 4 to 7 are seen to be irrelevant. They are simply "process"—the tendency to tell our reader how we proceeded, step by step. The reader doesn't need these steps. The finished product looks like this:

Revision

Orientation and facts: Veronica Larson has asked to be transferred to California on December 12, 1980. She'll be interviewed by Stuart Brown, Hillside personnel manager, for future openings.

Closing: Please give Veronica a 30-day relocation leave and send a copy of her original application to Mr. Brown.

Your subject heading can alert the reader to why you're writing. How can you adapt the subject of this memo?

Original

Subject: Budget Computerization

As we have previously discussed, Monarch Computer Services has provided a verbal bid for placing the budget and the allocation and expenditure activities related to the budget on the computer system.

Their estimate is $5,000 for the software package with related special reports. This expense is high because of the unique features which seem inherent in our system. The general ledger program which Monarch Computer Systems currently has would not be adaptable to our system, thus driving up the cost of this software package.

If you feel this is a reasonable price for the tasks you wish to accomplish, please contact Barbara (extension 404) so that planning meetings can be arranged with the representatives of the computer company.

On the basis of the activities you discussed and because of the uniqueness of our bookkeeping system, I think this is a reasonable price.

Purpose: To ask the reader whether we should computerize the budget or not.

Facts:

1. Monarch has bid $5,000 to computerize our budget.
2. This high expense stems from the unique features of our system, which is not adaptable to Monarch's general ledger system—the price seems fair.
3. If you agree, set up meetings through Barbara.

Revision

Subject: Should we computerize our budget system?

Monarch Computer Services has verbally bid $5,000 to provide this service. Since it will have to custom-design a system for us (its general ledger system doesn't adapt to our unique features), this price seems fair.

If you want to go ahead, please set up planning meetings through Barbara (extension 404).

Organizing Memos with Headings

This memo is disorganized and hard to follow.

Here is some material on the Houston Area Council-Capital Funding Campaign. The scouts are trying to raise $4,000,000 for improvements to the area camping facilities. They also want to have an Endowment Fund for Camperships so that more boys can have the opportunity to use the facilities.

The Houston Area Council (HAC) is divided into districts. We are in the Eagle District. We have the use of four camping facilities that belong to the council. They are:

Rapawom Scout Reservation—Yorkville
Matatou Camp—Laiborn
Seminate Reservation—Oswego
Fort Riley—North Chickapee

The Eagle district uses Fort Riley for most of the district events and troop outings and for all the training sessions the Council gives to leaders and boys alike.

The camp needs to replace much of the equipment that has been in use for several years now and is falling apart. Among these items are a one-ton truck, a tractor with snow-blowing and grass-cutting abilities, winterization of the cabin and lodge for year-round camping, new latrines, etc. Most of the other camping facilities are in need of the same equipment.

We can help make Camping more enjoyable for the Scouts by contributing to the Capital Campaign. The Boy Scouts need the money to continue their work and we have a say in the matter of how our money is to be used. The money that we pledge can be spread over a three-year period for payment.

The Houston Area Council will come and give a presentation for the Executives next week if it is convenient with your schedule. This subject was presented to the executive board and received concurrence. It was referred to you since only financial support is needed and the amount of money in question is beyond our budget appropriation.

Please call me if you feel we should contribute and whether to schedule a presentation.

The memo suffers from several weaknesses:

1. No planning—the ideas don't fall into any pattern or order and are hard to follow.
2. Lack of attention to the reader's needs—the memo doesn't say why it's addressed the reader until the end, and even then the purpose is not clear.
3. Too much verbiage—many of the details given are irrelevant, and the delivery itself could be shorter.
4. Poor emphasis—the paragraphs drone on without highlighting important ideas.
5. Weak structure—unnecessary capital letters and repetitions abound; rules of grammar are violated.

Once again, informational memos rely on a simple format: opening, middle, and closing. The first step is to determine why you're writing. You then list your facts. You order the facts according to the basic format, being sure to use headings to separate groups of ideas in the middle. It works like this:

Purpose: To inform your readers about the scouts' campaign so they'll know whether they want to contribute to it or not.

Opening (*orientation*):
1. As part of the Houston Area Council (HAC) capital funding campaign, the Boy Scouts want to raise $4,000,-000.
2. The executive committee wants to contribute, but it

needs your estimate of how much to contribute (if any-thing), since you deal with large requests for money and know what's feasible.

Middle (*facts*):
1. The money would be used for facilities improvement and camperships.
   a. Equipment—truck, tractor.
   b. Improvements—roads, cabins, latrines.
2. The contribution would be financed over three years and we'd have a say in how it's used.

Closing:
1. The HAC has offered to present its proposal next week to our executives.
2. Call me if you're interested.

These are the essential items the reader needs to know. Given the purpose of the memo, anything else is wasted at this point. The final product would read like this:

> You may be interested in our contributing to the Houston Area Council (HAC) campaign. The Council wants to raise $4,000,000 for the Boy Scouts. The executive committee needs your estimate of how much (if anything) to contribute.

Background Information

   Uses for money
   1. Equipment—one-ton truck, snow-blowing and grass-cutting tractor.
   2. Improvements—roads, cabins (winterization for year-round use), latrines.
   3. Camperships.

   Financing
   1. We can spread our contribution over three years.
   2. We'll have a say in how it's used.

The HAC has offered to present its proposal next week to our executives. Please call me if you're interested so I can set up a date convenient for you.

Alerting the reader to the factual section by introducing it with the heading "Background Information" is helpful. You must be careful, however, to make sure all groups of thoughts hang together.

When you write an informational memo containing many facts, block out the facts by paragraphs, each with its own heading. The design looks like this:

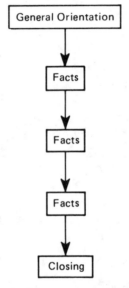

Each level of the discussion must develop logically from the preceding one. If you use numbers, letters, or headings in list form, you must clarify the relationships between ideas. The listed items must be introduced, and nothing can be included in your facts that doesn't relate to your overall introduction. If you're dealing with several different facts, the introduction must alert the reader to this. Finally, you should always move from general ideas to more specific facts. This next example doesn't hold together. The introduction and the facts don't relate logically.

Faulty Example

Original

To: All customer services representatives
Re: Cash and credit-card enrollments by phone

All customer services representatives will be responsible for taking cash and credit-card enrollments by phone. This is the information you must obtain:

Cash Enrollment
1. Name
2. Address and phone number
3. Mark the $33 box
4. Instruct members on receiving notification as to when to submit check

Some members may wish to enroll their children of driving age. If this is so, you must get the following information:

Associate Members
1. Name
2. Date of birth
3. Mark the $45 box

To enroll by major credit cards, the following information is necessary:

Major Cards
1. Number
2. Expiration date
3. Mark the $33 box

The categories A, B, and C don't logically act as dividers of thoughts. Also, the lists under these categories are not a parallel form—a source of confusion for the reader. The organization is clearer in this revised memo.

Revision

All customer services representatives should follow this procedure for taking cash or credit-card enrollments by phone.

Cash
1. For members
   ○ Get name, address, and phone number.
   ○ Mark the $33 box.
   ○ Tell them we'll notify them later about when to send their check.
2. For associate members (children of driving age)
   ○ Get name and date of birth.
   ○ Mark the $45 box.

Credit Cards
   ○ Get number and expiration date.
   ○ Mark the $33 box.

SAMPLE MEMOS AND REVISIONS

Each of these memos can be put into one of the formats discussed in this chapter, as illustrated in the revised forms.

Example 1

Original

Subject: Monthly Meeting

On a regular basis, it would be my desire that Sam Watson and I meet with you to keep you informed of the ongoing mailings that we will be doing in conjunction with your firm. I would recommend that the meetings be held on the third Tuesday of every month at 11:30 A.M. Furthermore, I would recommend that Steven White also sit in on these meetings. I perceive that some of the difficulties in expeditiously obtaining lists and in the processing of tapes could be eliminated as a result of these meetings.

Your kind consideration would be appreciated. Please advise if this is agreeable.

Revision
Format—Informational

I suggest you regularly meet with Sam Watson, Steven White, and me. We hope to accomplish these objectives:

1. Keep you informed of the mailings we'll be doing jointly with your firm.
2. Eliminate problems in getting lists and processing tapes.

Would the third Tuesday every month at 11:30 A.M. be convenient for you? Please let me know your thoughts next week.

Example 2

Original

The ABC project team, which was appointed on August 14, has completed its analysis of the 1978 Automative Review. It prepared its work plans, which outline tasks and man-day estimates; it recommended task force members; and it proposed an implementation schedule for each work plan. A copy of each of the preliminary work plans is attached for your inspection.

I fully recognize the need to move forward in correcting the problems pointed out by the Project Team. However, the 744 man-days of work needed according to the report would make meeting the October 20 beginning date difficult, since all personnel are currently involved in other tasks. By shifting priorities and working on only two work plans concurrently, the Automative Section can provide the necessary support to meet the implementation schedule in the report. Additional clerical staff would have to be provided also.

MIS would have to allocate resources to the project that are now committed to 30 other projects. Several of these are critical to accomplishing our goals for next year. To continue these and to begin the new schedule, MIS will need a minimum of one additional analyst.

A possible alternative is to authorize one MIS analyst from the 1981 budget.

Barney Baker is in favor of the project and the changes I suggest. Please get back to me by the end of the week to discuss it.

Revision
Format—Problem–Analysis–Solution

We have a problem concerning the ABC project team's analysis of the 1978 Automative Review. Their work plans outline tasks and schedules adding up to 744 workdays (see attached copy). To begin the project on time, however, other critical work would suffer.

To solve this problem, I suggest taking these measures (Barney Baker agrees):

1. The automative section should shift priorities and work on only two plans at the same time.
2. We should hire extra clerical personnel.
3. MIS should allocate resources from 30 other projects. Also, it should hire another analyst for this work, possibly authorizing one from the 1981 budget.

Please get back to me by Friday with your thoughts on this.

Example 3

Original

Attached are the original proposal and an additional proposal, offering two alternatives for additions to the repair shop.

I visited the repair shop Monday, and in my opinion something must be done if we are to operate the shop in a productive manner. It has been several years since I visited the repair shop, and I was appalled at the work and clutter I found compared to how it used to be. With the cramped space and heavy workload, we can't expect that group to be very efficient. Another thing that bothers me greatly is the lack of cranes capable of handling the large transformers we must repair. If Tony's safety group or OSHA were to go and observe some of the work practices, I think they would pull their hair out at the way we have to go about handling the equipment we repair.

As pointed out in this morning's staff meeting, we are charged by our stockholders with keeping their assets in first-class condition. I personally think we are derelict in showing accountability at the repair shop.

I would like to meet with you at an early date to discuss the need for additional space and equipment.

Revision
Format—Triangle Principle

I believe we should make the proposed space and equipment changes (attached) at our repair shop for these reasons:

1. The shop is cluttered and cramped (unlike the way it was when I first visited it). This makes work inefficient.
2. No cranes are available to handle the large transformers we repair.
3. Tony's safety group or OSHA may well object to our poor safety practices.

The sentiment expressed at this morning's staff meeting was apt: Our stockholders deserve better. Please call me within the next two weeks to set up a meeting on this.

Example 4

Original

Approximately 3½ weeks ago I put in a request to Marcia Riley to have a phone transferred from order processing to the shipping-distribution area.

Last week I requested that another phone be transferred from the same area. They have a surplus. Maggie Barton and I have discussed this and we are in full agreement.

These phones are needed to keep my department running smoothly and efficiently.

Revision
Format—Informational

Maggie Barton I have agreed that two phones should be transferred from order processing to the shipping-distribution area. This makes sense, since they have a surplus and we are short of supply.

After two requests (the first 3½ weeks ago, the second last week), I'm still waiting. Would you please speak to Marcia Riley in order processing and let me know what the cause of the delay is.

9

MINUTES
AND MEETING
SUMMARIES

An advantage of writing summaries or minutes (as opposed to telling what went on) is the time you have to organize your thoughts. You can use the space on the page effectively to highlight and emphasize what was important. The boring quality of most summaries is the repetition of who said what to whom. But there's no reason why you can't structure your writing so that the details don't lull the reader to sleep.

Compare the following two versions of the same minutes of a planning meeting.

Original

Those in Attendance: _____, _____, and _____
March 15, 1980

Dr. Smith suggested that each ALD identify a specific person responsible for coordination and preparation of the Institution Plan. There will be a meeting with these representatives on April 5 to discuss the Plan.

It was strongly suggested by Dr. Brown that we should be prepared to review for Dr. Jones which programs aren't working well. This discussion led to a suggestion by Mr. Alder that we should set aside a sum of money to put these programs back on target.

The suggestion was made by Ms. Davids to hire a consultant to ascertain why morale is so low among our support staff. As a result, Dr. Ingram will research possible firms and send Ms. Davids a memo within the next few weeks.

There being no further business, the meeting was adjourned at 2:00 P.M.

Respectfully submitted by _____

Revision

Date of Meeting;	March 15, 1980
Time Begun:	1:00 P.M.
Those Present:	_____, _____, and
	_____
Recording Secretary:	Joan Green
Time Ended:	2:00 P.M.

Suggestions:
1. Dr. Smith wants each ALD to select someone to coordinate/prepare the Institution Plan. He'll meet with the group on April 5.
2. Dr. Brown wants us to review for Dr. Jones which programs aren't working well. Mr. Alder suggests we set aside money to improve these programs.
3. Ms. Davids feels we should hire a consultant to find out why morale is low among support staff. Dr. Ingram will research possible firms and send her a memo within two weeks.

The facts of this communication could also be put into chart form, such as the one on the facing page. You can substitute any headings you want in this chart. Whether you use a chart or list, the items must be easy to read. The list should be in parallel form and should cover only items promised in the heading.

Note this summary and revision.

Original

April 20 meeting—WLIC operations and 1980 budget

Meeting highlights follow. Please let me know if any of these items do not reflect our discussion or if you desire to make amendments to them.

Suggestion	Person suggesting	Response or action resulting	Person responding
Each ALD should select someone to coordinate/prepare the Institution Plan.	Dr. Smith	Meeting between reps and Dr. Smith to be held on April 5.	
We should review for Dr. Jones which programs aren't working well.	Dr. Brown	We should set aside money for These programs.	Mr. Alder
We should hire a consultant to learn why support staff morale is low.	Ms. Davids	Dr. Ingram will research possible firms and send her a memo within two weeks	

Reporting Procedure
- Michael Kopel reports directly to David Hals until such time as a new Education Director is named.
- Hals approves expense accounts, leave or sick requests, budget revisions, and adjustments.
- Dick Gregory will provide Kopel with design concepts for eventual production by a Cleveland advertising firm. The printed materials will direct prospective students to MIC programs by encouraging them to use our toll-free number.
- Kopel will meet with Stanley Davis to coordinate the 800-number referral slips.

In this memo, the author uses "Reporting Procedure" to cover more than the category promises. Here's an improvement.

Revision

Meeting Highlights

1. Reporting
    a. Michael Kopel will report to David Hals until an education director is named.
    b. Hals will approve expense accounts, leave or sick requests, budget revisions, and adjustments.
2. Promotion
    a. Dick Gregory will give Kopel designs for future production by a Cleveland advertising firm. Materials will attract future MIC students by encouraging use of our toll-free 800 number.
    b. Kopel will meet with Stanley Davis to coordinate use of the 800-number referral slips.

Here's another example of alternative ways to summarize a meeting.

Original

The major revision in management is beginning to coalesce into an effective functionally oriented team. Areas of functional responsibility have been clearly reordered and two new functions, Marketing and Technical Services, have been accorded senior executive status. At this meeting, the newly ordered relationships between management functions were clearly described to a cross section of intermediate management people. An attitude reading suggests there is a substantial improvement in outlook and enthusiasm.

Introduction of a very promising High Performance Tool is progressing satisfactorily. A just completed survey indicates that these tools cut time on an average job by a great amount.

Our pricing tool strategies will be ready by May 15.

Revision

Areas of Discussion:

1. *Management Addition and Reordering*

  a. Functional responsibilities were reordered—two new functions, marketing and technical services, were given executive status.
  b. An attitude survey was taken—results show substantial improvement in outlook.
2. *High-Performance Tool*
  a. The tool has been doing well—survey shows it cuts time on an average job by a great amount.
  b. Our pricing strategy for the tool will be completed by May 15.

In this report, when you cut out the excess language, you once again find that little is actually said. These questions arise:

1. How were functional responsibilities reordered?
2. Who decided the functions were to have executive status and why?
3. How much is "substantial" outlook improvement?
4. How much is the "great amount" of time the new tool reduces?
5. What does "doing well" mean?

Try to anticipate and answer questions by dealing in specific terms. Be complete. Your readers want the facts spelled out, even if they attended the meeting.

10

REPORTS

Before writing a report, determine what your objective is and how best to achieve it.

Purpose—What do you want to accomplish (and should it be written at all)?

Audience—What is the reader required to know? Should the message be formal or casual? How detailed should it be?

Format—Justification, recommendation, progress, progress and justification, description.

When writing reports, pay careful attention to:

Logical sequence
Accuracy of data
Completeness
Separation of opinion from conclusion
Brevity and simplicity

Avoid generalizations. Be on the lookout for empty expressions such as these:

profit increase, superior product, cost improvement, quicker payout, time saved, lower depreciation, improved technology

BASIC FORMAT

Summary: Acts as a mini-report for those who are too busy to read the entire report. Puts conclusions up front because these are the central feature of the report. Includes

purpose of the report, scope of the problem, major conclusions and recommendations, and (optional) a short
statement about how the facts were obtained.

All parts of the summary should appear in the same
order as in the report to make for easy cross referencing.
You may use numerals and abbreviations; don't use
tables and graphs. Keep it short—about a page.

Introduction: Considers the background and experience of
the readers. Can give information needed to understand
the subject matter. The more widespread the readership,
the more explication is needed. However, don't dwell on
methodology. The conclusions are the central feature of
the report.

Includes definition of terms, explanation of technique
or process, limited historical background, and background of investigations (if relevant).

Body: Conclusions (already stated in summary) are ex-
pounded. You may outline recommendations, advantages, and disadvantages. You may also follow with a
supporting discussion. Some tables (short) may be included here for illustration.

Appendix: Statistics, working memos, tables, graphs, maps,
photographs, and so forth. You may include facts you
discarded as not essential to the main part of the report.

Sample Summary

Over the past four years, enrollment in the Smithover elementary school has grown so quickly that a new school is
needed. This report evaluates Greenacres as a possible site.
This evaluation is based on analysis of land cost, amount of
land available, physical characteristics, accessibility, population concentration, zoning, and safety factors.

Greenacres has these advantages:
1. The entire 217-acre plot can be bought for $800,000.

2. It's conveniently located, and it can easily be provided with sewers and utilities.
3. Access isn't hampered by traffic.
4. Zoning is adequate for building.
5. It serves a large concentration of families.

Greenacres has these two disadvantages:
1. A 50-acre swamp on the property needs draining.
2. About 50 residents have petitioned to keep the school off the plot so that property lines won't be disturbed.

Since the swamp can be drained easily, and since the property of local residents isn't directly affected by the proposed school, these problems can be handled without difficulty.

Conclusion: Greenacres is a favorable site for the school.

The summary begins with the purpose of the report, so that the reader immediately knows why the report has been written. I've seen many reports that never announce their purpose—the reader is left to guess. In the summary above, the purpose was to evaluate Greenacres.

The scope of the summary limits and defines what aspects of the subject you're actually handling. You should know the scope of the report before you begin collecting data for it. The Greenacres summary, for example, covered aspects from land cost to safety. Other elements have been left out, and the reader should be alerted to this. Among other things, the study doesn't discuss how much land is cleared or how far the site is from other existing schools.

The process of writing a report might be viewed as a series of steps:

1. Decide why you're writing; make sure the matter hasn't been covered already; if this is an assignment, clarify what is wanted.
2. State the problem you're dealing with.
3. Define the scope of the problem.

4. Plan your research.
5. Collect your information.
6. Form your conclusions.
7. Prepare a draft.
8. Edit to make the document as short as you can.

You may want to write your summary after you've finished the actual report. Remember, though, that the summary goes first and contains all the major items the reader should consider.

Two problems that occur often in report writing are faulty conclusions and too much time taken to justify negative conclusions. A faulty conclusion is likely when you fail to follow a thought process to its logical end. For example, you might conclude that a product has advantages over those of competitors on the basis of tests that didn't measure all criteria. Too much time taken to justify negative results reflects the problem we all have. We think the effect will be softened if we blanket an unpleasant message in many words. This principle holds true also for letter writing. Reports should be objective, unconcerned with the reader's feelings.

EXAMPLE OF ORIGINAL REPORT AND REVISION

Original

Introduction

We have completed our audit of the Wonderland Data Center in Germany, which provides support for certain computer applications of ABC Company. This audit was a first for us for several reasons, as follows:

○ First audit of a foreign computer facility
○ First audit of a new computer facility

This report contains our findings, recommendations, and comments relative to the activities and accomplishments of

Wonderland's Data Processing Department personnel. These findings and recommendations will be reviewed with auditors from the Mark Stone Company to avoid duplication of audit procedures at fiscal year end. We reviewed their first draft of the Billing System report.

The Wonderland installation consists of a Class C central processing unit, three magnetic tape drives, and one printer. In addition, the Data Center uses a telephone company message switching system for communications with sales offices and warehouses.

The organizational structure consists of 3 administrators, 12 operators, 1 secretary, and 1 technician. This organization will be revised after the newly formed steering committee has defined its plans.

Major Findings

This data center is in its infancy and is beginning to mature. Many good management philosophies are in place though not formalized. Very positive attitudes toward the company and departmental growth are quite apparent. Certain major weaknesses must be attended to before they become problems:

1. Departmental standards and procedures must be developed, published, implemented, and strongly enforced.
2. Experts in the areas of insurance, fire protection, and security should be sought to review current status and recommend necessary improvements.
3. Research of available software controls should be done.

Although the present installation is the first computer the company has had, we were pleased to note that many administrative and operational controls have been implemented. Some of the more significant findings are:

1. Responsibilities for various aspects of department functions have been assigned.
2. Adequate division of responsibilities has been developed.

3. Relatively secure computer center has been provided including most access control.
4. Manual tape management is implemented.
5. Excellent off-site storage facility for data media has been established.
6. Password protection is utilized for computer terminal applications.
7. A comprehensive billing system was developed and implemented.

There were some weaknesses noted. For example, formal departmental standards and procedures do not exist; no formal comprehensive disaster plan; insurance on equipment and facilities is needed; fire equipment is not sufficient; better external access security; software controls (library for programs, tape management); fire and evacuation plans; inadequate program documentation; formalized agreement for a back-up facility; and critical and sensitive reports and files need to be identified and protected.

Scope

This audit concentrated on an evaluation of administrative and operational controls as exercised by the different functional areas. Our basic guidelines were used in addition to the following measurements: review of the Mark Stone Data Center report; review of the Mark Stone Billing System report; review of the Internal Audit Billing System report.

Revision

Summary

Purpose: To reflect the findings of our audit of the Wonderland Data Center in Germany (which supports some of ABC Company's computer functions).

Scope: Using our audit guidelines, we evaluated controls (administrative and operational). We reviewed several Mark Stone Company reports (Data Center, Billing System, and Internal Audit Billing System) to avoid year-end duplication.

Findings:
Strengths
A. General
  1. This young center has good (though informal) management philosophy, positive attitudes, and growth potential.
  2. Departmental responsibilities have been assigned and division responsibilities developed.
  3. The center is relatively secure.
B. Specific
  1. The center has access control and uses password protection for computer terminals.
  2. Verbal reciprocal computer back-up agreements have been made; these need to be formalized, however.
  3. The center has a manual tape management system and excellent off-site data media storage.
  4. An in-house billing system has quickly been established.

Needs
  1. Departmental procedures
  2. Expert insurance security review and recommendations
  3. Fire equipment
  4. Disaster plan
  5. Better security over external access
  6. Protection of sensitive files and reports
  7. Software controls (program library and tape management)
  8. (See number B2 under "strengths")

Introduction

Background
This audit was a first as an audit in two areas: of both a foreign and a new computer facility.

Equipment
Current: a Class C central processing unit, three magnetic tape drives, and one printer;

also, a telephone company message switching system for communicating with sales offices and warehouses.

Planned: upgrade to a Class A processing unit; addition of a second printer.

Organization (to be revised after the steering committee defines its plans)

    3 administrators

    12 operators

    1 secretary

    1 technician

11

ADAPTING
YOUR STYLE

Whether you're writing for someone or to someone, always keep your reader in mind as you write. Some of the best communicators have learned the value of empathy, the ability to put oneself in another's place and see things through that other person's eyes. Behavioral scientists have adapted the work of Carl Jung on interaction. According to Jung, most people have a predominant personality style and at least one secondary style. Getting along with others is in part adapting yourself to any or all of these four styles.

Thinker: Tends to be conservative, methodical, and deliberate; loves data, charts, and graphs; won't act before carefully thinking a move through. *Stereotype:* Accountant.

Feeler: Is people-oriented, loyal and sensitive; enjoys socializing while discussing business; worries more about how each move will affect colleagues than about dollars and cents. *Stereotype:* salesperson.

Intuitor: Is a creative thinker, imaginative and forward-directed; enjoys dreams and five-year plans; hates to be pinned down. *Stereotype:* planner.

Doer: Is action-oriented; hates to waste time; wants to know immediately what the results will be; at times is brusque or impatient. *Stereotype:* executive.

To apply this knowledge, simply use your common sense. For example, think back to the memo about respirators. You were recommending their purchase for these reasons:

Employee benefits—morale and health

Company benefits—productivity, avoidance of strike, public relations

If you know you're trying to convince a Feeler, which of the two categories of benefits would you put first? Since the Feeler cares primarily about people, you'd stress employee benefits and put that category first. For the Doer, you'd emphasize company benefits. The Thinker would want to see carefully assembled data for every suggestion. Finally, for the Intuitor, you'd discuss long-range changes in the company's image. You wouldn't leave anything out: it's simply a question of what to accent. If you don't know what type of personality your reader has, include aspects that would appeal to any of the four.

In analyzing personality styles, I've found that most people work for someone whose predominant style is different than theirs. This is explained in part by the hierarchical nature of management. As you move up the managerial ladder, you tend to become more of a Doer, less of a Feeler or Intuitor. The difference is also explained by the old truism that opposites attract. People seem to work together best when they can complement each other's skills. The creative person needs to be prodded; the overly analytical thinker needs some aggressive opposition.

Another aspect of adapting your style comes into play when you're writing on behalf of someone else. If your supervisor is conservative and asks you to fill in, you don't have to be distant or cold when assuming the role. You simply have to analyze the components of your supervisor's writing and be slightly more formal than you might choose to be. The same thing works in reverse when you're adapting the style of someone more informal than you. The things to look for are use of contractions, simple words, personal pronouns, and direct questions.

SAMPLES

Your boss writes:

> I would like to invite you to our open business meeting on April 4. At that time you can see what we are doing to cut prices for you.
> I would appreciate your letting me know by March 19 whether you can attend.

The style here is somewhere between conservative and informal. In representing this person, be matter of fact and direct. Choose words that are simple and clear. Don't use too many contractions. Do use personal pronouns freely.

Your boss writes:

> You're in luck. Our next open meeting's set for April 4. Drop by and we'll show you our latest price-cutting techniques.
> John, please tell me by March 19 if you can make it. I hope to see you there.

Obviously this person is highly informal. Try to think of your reader as a friend you're talking to as you imitate this free, open style.

Your boss writes:

> This is to advise that an open meeting has been scheduled for April 4. If you care to attend, we will acquaint you at that time with the various techniques we are incorporating in order to reduce prices.
> Please advise of your attendance by March 19. Thanking you in advance, I remain. . . .

Again, don't write in this pompous fashion to represent someone else. Compromise. Be a little more formal than you might choose to be without sacrificing the principles of good business writing.

Checklist

Does the person you're representing
    Use contractions?
    Begin with the "you" attitude?
    Refer to the reader by name?
    Ask direct questions?
    Use stereotyped expressions?
    Use lists to organize?
    Show warmth and friendliness?
    End in a positive way?

12

MARKETING YOURSELF

Writing a résumé is not a one-dimensional process. What you say and how you say it depend on what you want to accomplish. The same person may write several résumés, depending on the job being applied for at the time. For one job you might stress one group of strengths, for another job a different group.

GENERAL POINTS

1. Keep your objective in mind. If you're asking for a particular job, focus on skills associated with what that job calls for.
2. Don't tell everything. Be selective so that you don't numb the reader with details. After a while, your attributes lose distinction and value if you outline too many.
3. Organize selectively. If you want to impress with your educational credentials rather than your job experience, list your schooling first. If, on the other hand, your work background tells the story, begin with that. Put in more details about your most recent job, fewer about your earliest work experiences.
4. Stress concrete responsibilities rather than vague abstractions. Don't use big words. State in simple, specific terms what you have done and can do.
5. Don't mention the salary you want. You may get a better offer than you anticipate asking for.

6. Don't put down specific references. Wait for someone to be interested in actually hiring you so that the people on your list don't get tired of recommending you to no purpose.
7. If possible, write a specific résumé for each job you apply for, showing how your credentials fit the requirements of the job.
8. Begin by stating what your job objective is, either in general or in specific terms.

Model

Name: Richard D. Shawn
Address: 20 Allendale Road, Middletown, New York 10067
Phone: (914) 546-9087

Career Objective: Principal of an urban high school

Employment:
September 1978–June 1980
  Randolph Heart High School, New York, New York; assistant principal.
  I was responsible for all ninth- and tenth-grade discipline. I acted as liaison between guidance department and students.
September 1964–June 1978
  Public School 142, Brooklyn, New York; teacher of eighth-grade mathematics.
  I designed the curriculum for the eighth-grade math program. Also, I started a successful "rap clinic" for students with discipline problems.
September 1962–June 1964
  I worked part-time as a youth guidance counselor for an inner-city drug rehabilitation program.

Education
1962 M.A. Boston University. Psychology and Education major.
1960 B.A. University of Maryland. Education major.

References
Available if requested.

Another approach is to describe your general skills immediately after stating your career objective. The following example, which illustrates this approach, must be revised to clean up the verbiage.

Original

Career Objective	Management/Administrative position which will allow me to utilize my extensive experience and skills in a challenging environment.
SKILLS	
Management	Responsibility for four medical services consisting of over 300 patient beds and two intensive care units. Responsibility for the twenty-four-hour operation of the Duty Office, which has administrative control of a 1,200-bed hospital on evenings, nights, and weekends. Administrative liaison with all centralized departments in order to ensure efficient provision of hospital services. Coordinated programs with various levels of staff and community agencies. Responsibility for assuring compliance with all applicable codes and standards, including government regulations. Active in risk management policies. Determined workload of staff and type of service to be provided. Policy and procedure development.

Program Development and Evaluation/Operations Analysis	Devised and implemented new statistical reporting forms and analyses. Conducted quality assurance activities, including audits and research studies. Planned, organized and supervised outreach programs involving four community agencies. Initiated, organized, and successfully developed a new type of treatment program. Analyzed and modified operational procedures. Developed operational manuals.
Personnel	Supervised professional and nonprofessional staff. Created and implemented training programs for administrative, professional, and nonprofessional personnel. Participation in labor relations and grievance proceedings. Lectured to audiences with varied levels of education and experience. Recruited and interviewed potential staff and made final decision on hiring. Performed employee evaluations. Conducted public relations and fund-raising campaigns.

Revision

Career Objective: Management/Administrative Position
SKILLS

Management Responsibilities
- Four medical services (over 300 beds and 2 intensive care units).
- Twenty-four-hour duty office with control of 1,200-bed hospital.

- Liaison with all central departments.
- Coordination of staff and community agencies.
- Risk management; policy and procedure development; purchase of equipment and supplies.

Program Development—Evaluation/Operations
- Devised statistical reporting forms and analyses.
- Conducted audits and research studies.
- Planned and developed outreach programs with four community agencies.
- Developed new treatment program and operational manual.

Personnel
- Developed training programs.
- Participated in labor and grievance proceedings.
- Lectured.
- Recruited and interviewed; made final hiring decisions.
- Conducted public relations and fund-raising campaigns.

Another way to market yourself is by setting your goals on paper. Try to organize the document in a logical pattern, as the revision to this weak memo does.

Original

This memorandum is intended to address the issue of my career development. I would like to begin by saying that I feel comfortable working with you and the EB-VT group but as we discussed, I would like your support in promoting my career development.

I have for the last several years been preparing myself for transition into a professional position. Working in EB-VT affords me the opportunity to see job descriptions which surface, and as I read them I have attempted to appraise them to determine if my abilities and the tasks required to perform in that capacity are suited to each other.

The recent job description about which we spoke seems

like a good fit to me. That kind of position would allow me to utilize and develop the talents I now possess and broaden my total scope.

As you know, I have worked here for four (4) years in the Real Estate Division. During that time I rose from a Grade 7 Secretary to a Grade 9—two promotions in less than three (3) years. My responsibilities were mostly administrative and I was involved in all of the transactions made. I spent a good deal of time talking to brokers and potential purchasers. My job responsibilities there and previously were geared toward organization and coordination of business efforts. I have become extremely schedule-conscious, with a strong sense of priority and timing. Working in the real estate division sharpened my ability to work effectively under high pressure conditions because there were so many deadlines to be met and numerous preparations to make prior to closings.

Revision

Although I've been comfortable working with you and the EB-VT group, as we discussed I would like your support in furthering my career. The recent job opening we talked about seems like a good fit for me. Would you please give me your opinion on the basis of this background information:

Work Experience

In my four years in the real estate division, I went from Grade 7 secretary to Grade 9 (two promotions in less than three years). My actual duties were administrative, including responsibility for _____. [At this point you would want to be specific in outlining what you did].

Strengths

Working in real estate sharpened my ability to work under pressure, because of the many closings and preparations before closings. [Again, you would go on to give specifics about your strengths.]

The key to selling yourself in this kind of situation is avoiding all the nonsense talk ("I would like to begin," "I have attempted to appraise them," "I have been preparing myself for transition") and concentrating on facts. Your readers want to know what you can do, not what you think. They also want to see this at a glance, so your design is important. Don't think you'll impress anyone simply by covering pieces of paper with words. It's what you can do, not what you can say you can do, that counts. Finally, don't be too legalistic or pedantic by putting numbers both in written form and in parentheses. Once will suffice.

13

PROCEDURE MANUALS

Organizing company policy in book form can meet many objectives for you. For example, you can provide uniform procedures, reduce confusion and error, shorten training time, and eliminate arguments. The manual might contain these items:

1. Statement of purpose
2. Description of the scope
3. Contents page
4. Procedures or instructions
5. Copies of forms referred to in text

For the procedures or instructions, you would probably want to leave space at the top of each page for some or all of these categories.

Subject—this could include a subtitle.
Procedure number—put this in the upper right-hand corner.
Dates—when issued and when effective.
Supersedes—used to cancel a former instruction.
Approvals—space for one or several initials, depending on degree of complication.
Distribution—quantity agreed on; this could be a code the mailing service can use or a list to be checked off.
Applicability—tell each department whether it's appropriate for them.
Pages—each page of each instruction needs a number; page — of —.

Revision—this could be placed next to a revised passage or it could be a mark made in a box at the top.
Forms used—also, *forms no longer used.*

Here is an example of a possible format.

Subject   S.P. number

supersedes	s. p. no.	dated	pages	page number date effective
applicable to				date issued

app. by

One of the biggest problems in manual writing is the referencing system you use to ensure uniformity. Classification generally involves a coded system to save space. You might label each department with a different letter. Your instructions would have numbers broken down to individual divisions. For example, the general subject would be assigned the number 1. Secondary subjects could be 1.1 and 1.2 or even 1.1.1 and 1.1.2. The actual indexing would include both departments and subject matter, and the same concept might be listed more than once. Thus you could have an entry for accounting procedures, and at another point you could reference tax forms alphabetically.

Each manual needs some kind of control. You must decide who will get what, and you must make provisions for delivery. Not following instructions is as common as following them. Some of the failures are caused by lack of education; you must instruct employees about the existence and use of the manual. Other failures can be traced to deficiencies in the language and design of the document. If you write too much or set your words poorly on the page, the response will be to ignore them.

Don't overlook charts as a way of giving instructions.

You can adapt the headings to fit almost any requirement. For example, this chart would explain how to take telephone and regular orders.

Subject	Action	Example
Telephone orders	Take down relevant information Remind customer of July 4–9 sale days	Name, account number
Regular orders	Fill out order form find out how customer heard of us	Newspaper, TV ad, friend

Here are three poorly written procedures and their revisions for you to study.

SAMPLE ONE

Original

Handling Incoming Calls

Your main priority as a Customer Service Rep is to handle incoming calls from our members. You should answer the phone immediately when it rings and make the customer feel like you are there to only help him. Try to help the customer to the best of your knowledge and make him feel that his problem is being handled promptly. Remember, a call is not an interruption of your work but your first responsibility, so answer with a smile.

Telephone calls from members requesting travel information should *not* be handled by a Customer Service Rep. The reason for this is the fact that we do not have complete travel information regarding vacation planning. Calls cannot be

transferred to the Vacation Counseling desk, so please refer
members to call the toll-free numbers for the Vacation Department:

1. National 800-621-5412
2. Illinois 800-972-5565

Customers who call who are not club members, should *not*
be given the phone numbers of the Vacation Counseling
Desk. Travel information is a club benefit that members are
paying for, and this fact should be explained to the customer. It is important to stress the club benefits in a conversation of this nature. If the customer is looking for price
comparisons, send a brochure with the price comparison
charts. These charts are not 100% accurate because of continuous price increases; however, when our price increases
so does the regular price.

Every incoming phone call received by a CSR must be recorded. Calls are to be recorded on the telephone activity
summary sheet (see sample 1). At the top of the sheet, every
incoming call must be recorded by a slash mark. After handling a call, it is then necessary to summarize the call into
one of the categories listed on the lower part of the sheet.
This report is kept on a daily basis and turned into the Senior Rep weekly, who summarizes the sheets into a weekly
report. The Customer Service Manager and Operations
Manager utilize the report to determine trends in the club
and also to make improvements in the club's operation.

If an action is requested by the caller, it is necessary to fill
out the Telephone Request Form (see sample 2). This sheet
must be filled out *completely* so the appropriate action can
be taken. It is also necessary to indicate the action needed
and in the case of a cancellation/credit, the reason for can-
cellation/credit. These sheets should be placed in the daily
call basket so that the control clerk can re-route the call
sheet to the proper CSR for handling. Urgent Vacation Department call backs should be given to the Customer Service
Manager or Business Manager for immediate handling.

Revision

Handling Incoming Calls

Things to do

1. Take calls from our members
   Remember to answer the phone immediately and to
   make the customer feel you're happy to help him
2. Record all calls on the telephone activity summary sheet
   (see sample)
   Also, do the following:
   a. summarize the call——
   b. keep the report on a weekly basis
   c. turn report in to ——
      (———— and ———— will use these reports to
      ——)
3. Fill out telephone request form (sample 2) for any action
   requested by caller
   follow this procedure:
   a. ——
   b. ——

Things NOT to do

1. Don't handle travel information requests (we don't have
   complete information on this). Since these calls can't be
   referred to ———, ask callers to use the toll-free numbers for the Vacation Dept. (National ———, illinois
   ——)
2. Don't give customers who aren't club members the numbers of the Vacation Counseling Desk phones. Explain
   this is a club benefit for which members pay. Send anyone interested a price comparison chart (mention price
   fluctuations).

SAMPLE TWO

Original

1. Claims are received in batches from CRT
   Operator

2. Run tape on each claim within a batch
3. Record this total on Batch Control sheet
   and sign initials See Page 32
4. To balance pull up a PA11 See Page 44
   a. Sign on Terminal
   b. Use Identification Number
   c. Use Correct Password
5. Key in Batch Number, Total number of
   claims in a batch and the total amount of
   that batch.
   a. If correct, the screen will display In Balance
   b. If not correct the screen will display
   error in amount with a full display of
   claims inputed in that particular batch.
6. To locate the error, check screen against
   tape, reading the screen left to right which
   will show claim Number and the amount.
   When error is found correct the tape and
   Batch Control sheet and also make corrections on the screen.
7. When balancing is completed and you
   want to verify that all batches have been
   processed—pull up PA12 See Page 45
8. If all batches are in balance the screen will
   display Total number batches and total
   amount of all claims input for the day.

Revision

Action	Page	Extra
Get claims in batches from CRTs		
Run tape on each claim, record total on batch control, and initial control	32	
Balance by pulling up a PA11	44	sign on terminal use ID no. use correct password
Key in batch number, total claims, and total batch amount		if correct, screen will show "In Balance" if incorrect, screen will show error with full claim display
Find errors by checking screen against tape, reading left to right		
Correct error—correct tape and batch control sheet; correct the screen		
After balance complete, verify processing of all batches by pulling up PA12	45	
If all batches in balance, the screen will display total number of batches and amount of claim input for the day		

SAMPLE THREE

Original

Referral Code	Description and Override Procedures
N	Inactive Member—with code N Disablement date prior to effective date
	Override if:
	A. Disablement date is earlier than cancellation date e.g. Disablement Date 2/5/78 Effective Date 2/8/78 B. Disablement date up to 30 days prior to effective date
	e.g. Disablement Date 2/1/78 Effective Date 2/21/78
	Denial if:
	A. Disablement date is later than cancellation date e.g. Disablement Date 2/8/78 Effective Date 2/5/78 B. Disablement date more than 20 days prior to effective date e.g. Disablement Date 1/30/78 Effective Date 2/20/78
A	Address Different—address other than on file
	Override if:
	A. No obvious fraud Initiate a computer letter to respective CSC informing them of the change of address on this account.

Revision

Code	Subject	Action	Condition	Example
N	inactive member	override	if disablement date earlier than cancellation date	d.d. 2/5 c.d. 2/8
			if disablement date up to 30 days before effective date	d.d. 2/1 e.d. 2/21
		denial	if disablement date later than cancellation date	d.d. 2/8 c.d. 2/5
A	address different from on file	override	if there is no obvious fraud	
		write to tell CSC of address change for this account		

14

SUMMING IT UP

You now realize that writing is relatively simple if you approach it systematically. The process looks like this:

1. Decide why you're writing—what do you want your writing to induce your reader to do, think, or feel?
2. Collect and list your facts—think about your audience as you decide what to say. How detailed should you be? What is likely to motivate this reader? Do you want to sound warm and friendly?
3. Evaluate all facts in light of your purpose in writing— whatever you find to be irrelevant should be crossed out.
4. Organize your material in conformance with this sequence: Orientation, Facts, Closing. If you have many facts, work out headings. Decide where each paragraph should begin, and write a topic sentence for each.
5. Write your first draft.
6. Edit what you have written.
7. Write your final copy.
8. Proofread it.

Sample

Purpose: To get a refund for Mark Smith, who has canceled his registration for a seminar.

Facts:
1. Mark Smith is Director of Personnel Administration for ABC company.

2. He was registered to attend a seminar on Equal Employment Opportunities to be held on June 14 and 15, 1979, in New York.
3. The registration fee and tuition of $560, as indicated on Invoice 2234, has already been paid.
4. On June 11, I called to cancel Mr. Smith's registration for the above-mentioned seminar. The cancellation number given me was 77890. I was informed I should write to reader directly in order to receive a refund. Thus, this letter.
5. Please make the refund check out to Mark Smith and send it to the address given above.

Reorganized according to the prescribed sequence, it looks like this:

Orientation: I'm writing about a refund of payment for a canceled registration.

Facts: To be listed.

Closing: I want check sent to Mr. Smith.

Final copy

On June 11, I called you to cancel a registration for a seminar. Here is the background information:

Name of Participant:	Mark Smith (Director of Personnel Administration for ABC Company)
Seminar Title:	Equal Employment Opportunities
Date and Place:	June 14 and 15, 1979, in New York City
Total Fee:	$560
Cancellation Number:	77890

Please send a refund check for $560 payable to Mark Smith to the address listed above. Address the letter to my attention.

Thank you for your help.

EDITING

Editing should be approached systematically. If you know what your weaknesses are, you can look for and correct them. Make a personal checklist. For example, each time you find a mistake in your writing (or someone else brings it to your attention), put it on your list. Do you confuse *their, there,* and *they're?* Do you write *accept* when you mean *except?* Put them on your list.

The more attention you give to it, the larger your list will be. Here's how it might look at the beginning.

Checklist

Rules of grammar	1. Commas after introductory clauses.
	2. Semicolons with words like "however" and "therefore" when they join independent clauses.
	3. Agreement between subject and verb.
Usage	1. Difference between "infer" and "imply."
	2. Difference between "affect" and "effect."
Spelling	*receive, accommodate, judgment.*
Conciseness	Reword *there are* and *it is* constructions. Change these:
	I am of the opinion
	I would appreciate it if you would
	in the process of
	in the event that
	in the sum of
Informality	Begin with "you" approach. Use I and we.
Structure	Divide into orientation, facts, and closing.

When you edit, try speaking the words aloud or having them read to you by a friend. Or put your writing away for a few hours to separate your mind from word patterns that have become obsessive and therefore out of reach of your critical faculty.

When you proofread, read from the bottom of the page up. If you do this, you'll read for mistakes rather than for sense. The mind can pick up only a limited number of units at a glance. Consider this chart of your visual span:

A
AB
ABC
ABCD
ABCDE
ABCDEF

Words with six or more letters are hard to take in at a glance. You're likely to overlook a mistake in such words. Keep that in mind if you're tempted to skim through your copy quickly.

Taking pride in your work is important, both for you and for your organization. Don't sign anything you can't be proud of.

15

TEST YOURSELF

A. Correct any errors in grammar, punctuation, or usage.

1. The man who sat between Jane and I seemed sober but we couldn't be sure.
2. I appreciate you coming in early, however, you forgot to make the coffee.
3. The education and experience of each candidate was evaluated.
4. Neither the child nor the parents are expected to know the answers.
5. To get ahead in business, an effort must be made to work hard.
6. The condition caused her more trouble than she had expected, it caused her skin to pucker.
7. Shakespeare's play, *Hamlet,* is my favorite.
8. Irregardless of your attempts, you won't pass the test.
9. He payed my bill, but I still couldn't forgive him.
10. These kind of envelopes don't close well.
11. This is the most unique product on the market.
12. She typed with either a three or four inch margin.
13. The climate here is like Southern California.
14. Writing feverishly, the report met the deadline.
15. Do you mean to tell me neither of the soloists are able to play?
16. This strange phenomena puzzled the scientist.
17. The manager, as well as the president, feel sure he knows what to do.
18. I think it is time to affect a change in our government.
19. We enjoyed meeting with Mr. Brown and yourself.

20. A series of articles on drug abuses have been printed.
21. A small amount of people showed up.

B. Revise this letter.

Your letter regarding conduit requirements for telephone cable for new buildings 441 and 551 was referred to our Plant Engineering Facilities group. They informed us that building 441 is scheduled to be completed in April 1981 and building 551 is scheduled to be completed in July 1981. However, funding for these projects will not be available until after October 1, 1980. They plan to complete the drawings during October and have them ready by November 1, 1980. The actual construction work is scheduled for January 1981.

C. Make this list parallel.

When we begin setting up the Price Index System for including XYZ, we must do the following:

1. Any clodes assigned and checked against ABC must be included in ABC.
2. Major operating groups must be chosen.
3. I am assuming that all XYZ sales will be captured during the fourth quarter in 1980.

D. Correct the use of transitions in these two examples.

1. My division secretary is consistently late for work; however, her other work habits aren't a problem.
2. Gerry and I enjoyed your demonstration yesterday. You presented the problem well and answered every possible question. Before you came to the office, we were considering adding more machinery, but at this time we are not in a position to lease your equipment.

E. Shorten this letter.

This is in reply to your letter of April 17 concerning the amount of seminar announcements you are receiving from our organization.

I have processed a formal request to our Computer Facility to remove the duplicate and incorrect records in question from our files.

We have taken positive steps to reduce the amount of misguided mail by using the latest computer technology available for our promotional mailing programs. We have developed a mailing-list data base which now includes 85% of the lists we use.

In its simplest form, data base programming allows us to merge the four million names we regularly mail our literature to into one central file. Each file is then matched against every other file, and duplicate records are eliminated. However, unless the name and addresses are exactly the same, the computer is unable to match that record and eliminate it as a duplicate listing.

Obviously the system is not 100% perfect, but we do believe we have taken decisive steps to decrease the amount of unwanted mail.

Our deletion process does take twelve weeks to complete. Unfortunately, we cannot guarantee that you will not continue to receive our pamphlets during this time period because of advance preparation of labels and normal mail delivery.

We have every reason to believe that you will see the results of our efforts once the system has had a "chance to catch up with itself." If you should require further assistance during this time period, please do not hesitate to contact me.

Thank you for your cooperation, and we appreciate your taking the time to return the mailing pieces to us.

Possible Corrections

A. *Grammar, punctuation, usage*

1. The man who sat between Jane and me seemed sober, but we couldn't be sure.
2. I appreciate your coming in early; however, you forgot to make the coffee.

3. The education and experience of each candidate were evaluated.
4. Correct as is.
5. To get ahead in business, one must work hard.
6. The condition gave her more trouble than she had expected; it caused her skin to pucker.
7. Shakespeare's play *Hamlet* is my favorite.
8. Regardless of your attempts, you won't pass the test.
9. He paid my bill, but I still couldn't forgive him.
10. These kinds of envelopes don't close well.
11. This product is unique.
12. She typed with a three- or four-inch margin.
13. The climate here is like Southern California's.
14. Writing feverishly, he met the report deadline.
15. Do you mean to tell me neither of the soloists is able to play?
16. These strange phenomena puzzled the scientist.
17. The manager, as well as the president, feels sure he knows what to do. (Both the manager and the president feel sure they know what to do.)
18. I think it is time to effect a change in our government. (I think it is time to change our government.)
19. We enjoyed meeting with Mr. Brown and you.
20. A series of articles on drug abuses has been printed.
21. A small number of people showed up.

B. *Organization*

Our plant engineers (to whom your letter was referred) have given us this schedule for conduit requirements for telephone cable.

(a) Funding will be available after October 1, 1980.
(b) The drawings will be completed in October, and ready by November 1, 1980.
(c) The actual construction is scheduled to begin in January 1981.
(d) Building 44 should be completed in April 1981, building 551 in July 1981.

C. Parallelism

Change item C to "All XYZ sales must be captured during the fourth quarter of 1980."

D. Transitions

1. Although my division secretary is consistently late for work, her other work habits aren't a problem.

   or (changing the emphasis)

   Although her other work habits aren't a problem, my division secretary is consistently late for work.

2. Gerry and I enjoyed your presentation yesterday. Unfortunately, however, we've just decided against leasing any equipment right now. We'll certainly contact you if our plans change.

E. Conciseness

Thank you for telling us about the ecessive number of seminar announcements we've been sending you. We certainly plan to correct this problem for you.

We're using data base programming for our mailing. This system should correct most duplicate mailings, although once in a while we have a problem with matching names and addresses. I have asked our programmers to check on your file. You should see no more duplicates after the three months it takes to delete extra names.

If at that time you are still receiving duplicates, please write to me again. Meanwhile, I appreciate your writing to let us know about the situation.

APPENDIX

WORD CONFUSIONS

ability—power to do some-
thing
capacity—ability to hold, contain, or absorb

accent—emphasis
ascent—going up
assent—consent

access—way of getting in
excess—going beyond limits

adverse—hostile, opposed
averse—unwilling

affect (noun)—stilted; don't
use it
affect (verb)—to influence
effect (noun)—result
effect (verb)—to cause or
bring about

agree—to a proposal
on a plan
with a person

all right—always two words

already—earlier, previously
all ready—all of us ready

altar—place of worship
alter—change

altogether—completely
all together—as one group

anxious—worried
eager—desirous

anyway—anyhow
anyways—don't use it

appraise—judge
apprise—inform

being as—don't use this to replace since

beside—by the side of
besides—moreover

biannual—twice a year
biennial—every two years

breadth—distance or width
breath—an output of air
breathe—to take in or exhale
air

cannot help but—double negative
can't hardly—double negative

choose—present tense
chose—past tense

cite—to quote or mention
site—location

clothes—what we wear
cloths—pieces of material

compare to—point out differences by analogy

compare with—look for like-nesses

comprehensible—understandable

comprehensive—including a great deal

continual—close or rapid suc-cession

continuous—without interrup-tion

conveyer—person
conveyor—machine

discreet—prudent
discrete—separate

disinterested—unbiased, not influenced by personal rea-sons
uninterested—not interested

disregardless—don't use

envelop—to cover, wrap
envelope—covering, as for a letter

farther—measurable distance
further—all other uses

field test—noun
field-test—verb

first hand—noun
firsthand—adjective

forego—go before
forgo—go without

full time—noun
full-time—adjective

imply—suggest a meaning hinted at, give information
infer—draw conclusion, take in information

incredible—unbelievable
incredulous—unbelieving

irregardless—don't use

kind of a—leave out "a"

loose—not tightly fastened
lose—to suffer a loss
loss—defeat or misplacement

might of—should be "might have"

over all—adverb
overall—adjective

paid—past participle of pay
payed—only in sense of payed out rope or cable

part time—noun
part-time—adjective

personal—individual
personnel—staff

principal (adjective)—major, most important
principal (noun)—sum of money or chief person
principle (always a noun)—rule or doctrine

prophecy—noun
prophesy—verb

reason why—omit why

shut down—verb
shutdown—noun

stationary—fixed or unmoving
stationery—paper

than—use in making comparison
then—use for time

year end—noun
year-end—adjective

would of—should be "would have"

WORD USAGE

1. if/whether

   if—used to express conditions.
   Example: If you are late, we'll get caught in traffic.

   whether—shows doubt or is used in indirect questions.
   Example: I wonder whether he will arrive on time.
   I asked whether the men had arrived.

2. said— jargon when used as in "said person."
   same—legal use only, as in "payment for same."
   such— shouldn't be used in place of a demonstrative, as in "I won't tolerate such." Also, shouldn't be used as an intensive, as in "He is such a good worker."

3. these kind/those sort—kind and sort are singular; should be this sort or kind, these kinds or sorts.

4. Indefinite they—don't say:
   They have good corn in this state.
   They say taxes will never be reduced.

5. Indefinite it—don't say:
   In this book it says people live longer these days.

6. Dangling modifiers—clauses and phrases should clearly relate to the elements they modify.

   Wrong: To get to work on time, the bus should be caught at the corner.
   Right: To get to work on time, you should catch the bus at the corner.

   Wrong: Being the first woman executive here, my position is precarious.
   Right: Being the first woman executive here, I'm in a precarious position.

Wrong: When running down the street, the sun blinded him.

Right: When running down the street, he was blinded by the sun.

Wrong: As the secretary of our club, the robe clearly belongs to her.

Right: As the secretary of our club, she should have the robe.

7. Vague reference—clarify a statement when a pronoun can have two antecedents.

   Weak: The foreman told the worker he would work late.
   Better: The foreman told the worker to work late.

8. Comparison—use the comparative with two, the superlative with more than two.

   Right: He is the better worker of the two.
   She is the best worker in the office.

   Wrong: She is taller than any worker in the office.
   Right: She is taller than any other worker in her office.

9. Pronouns
   Subject case: I, you, he, she, they, who
   Object case: me, you, him, her, them, whom

   Right: I sat between Mary and her.
   He shared the candy among all of them.
   To whom did you send the invitation?
   They gave the flowers to Susan and me.
   Who did you say will make the speech?

10. Number and amount

    Number—for items that can be counted.
    A great number of people walked in at the same time.
    Amount—for quantity in bulk.
    I owed a great amount of money.

11. myself/me; yourself/you—only you can deal with yourself, as in "I looked at myself in the mirror."

Wrong: He met with John and myself.
   I spoke to Barbara and yourself on October 2.

Right: He met with John and me.
   I spoke to Barbara and you on October 2.

12. The possessive before -ing verb forms used as nouns; the objective case before -ing verb forms used as adjectives.

Right: I appreciate your coming here today.
   I don't like your behaving like a spoiled child.
   I would appreciate your doing it as soon as possible.
   I heard him singing in the shower.
   I saw them behaving like spoiled children.

13. its/it's

its—possessive: The dog wagged its tail.
it's—contraction: It's a beautiful day today.

WORDS MOST COMMONLY MISSPELLED

A

abbreviate
absence
abundance
accessible
accommodate
acknowledgment
advantageous
advice (noun)

advise (verb)
affidavit
allotment
allotted
all right
analogous
analyze
apologize

appearance
apropos
arrangement
assistance
assurance
attendance
authoritative
auxiliary

B

benefited
benevolent
best seller

bookkeeper
bulletin

bureau
business

C

calendar
caliber
canceled
cancellation
catalog
catchword
censure
ceremony
changeable
characteristic

chargeable
chiefly
choose
chose (past tense)
clientele
column
commission
commitment
committed
committee

commodities
comparative
compelled
competence
competitive
complementary
  (no charge)
complimentary
  (kind words)
concede

conceivable
conferred
confidential
conscientious
conscious
consensus
consul
convenience
co-op

cooperate
copyright
copywriter
corollary
correctable
correlation
council
counsel (advice)
counselor

counterfeit
courteous
courtesy
creditor
criticism
criticize
currency
customary

D

deceive
decision
deductible
defense
deferred
deficient
deficit
definite
definitely

dependent
desirable
devastate
development
diagramed
dictionary
difference
dilemma
diligent

disappearance
disastrous
discernible
discrepancy
diseases
dismissal
dissatisfied
dominant

E

earnest
echelon
eighth
eligible
embarrassment
emergency
eminent
employee
enclose
encouragement
enforceable
enlightenment

envelope
equally
equilibrium
equipped
equitable
equivalent
erroneous
essence
eventually
exaggerated
exceed

excellence
excerpt
exchangeable
excusable
exemption
exercise
exhaust
exhilarate
existence
exorbitant
extremely

F

facetious
familiar
fascinate
favorable
feasible
financial
flexible

fluorescent
focused
forcible
foreign
foreword
forfeit
formally

formerly
fortunate
fourth
frantically
frequently
fulfill
fundamental

G

gamut
gauge
generally
glamorous

glamour
glossary
government
grammar

grateful
grievance
guarantee
guidance

H

handicapped
handsome
harass
hazard
headache

height
helpful
hesitant
hindrance

homogeneous
humorous
hurriedly
hypothetical

I

idiosyncrasy
illegal
illegible
illicit
immaterial
immigrant
imminent
inaccessible

inaugurate
incidentally
incomparable
independent
inducement
inexhaustible
infinite
inherent

innocence
inoculate
inquiry
insignificant
installment
interfered
irresistible
itinerary

J

jealousy	judgment	juvenile
jeopardize	judicial	

K

kernel	know-how	knowledge
kidnaper		

L

labeled	leveling	loneliness
laboratory	library	loose (adjective)
latter	license	lose (verb)
legible	lightening	lying
leisure	livelihood	

M

maintenance	medicine	misinterpreted
manageable	medieval	misspell
mandatory	mediocre	monotonous
maneuver	merchandise	morale
meant	miscellaneous	mortgage
medal	mischievous	municipal

N

naive	negligible	ninety
naturally	neighbor	noticeable
necessary	niece	nucleus
necessitate	nineteenth	numerous

O

obsolescence
obsolete
occur
occurred
occurrence

occurring
offered
often
omitted
opinion

ordinance (rule,
    decree)
originate
outrageous

P

paid
pamphlet
parallel
paralyze
paraphernalia
parliamentary
pastime
patience
peaceable
peculiar
perceive
performance
permanent
permissible
permitting
perseverance
persistence

personnel
pertinent
pessimistic
phenomenon
physical
plausible
pleasant
possession
practically
precedence
predominant
preferable
preference
preferred
prejudice
preparation
prerequisite

presence
prevalent
privilege
procedure
proceed
processor
proficient
profited
programmed
prominent
promissory
pronunciation
pseudonym
psychiatry
psychology
pursue

Q

qualitative
quantitative
quarantine

quarreled
questionnaire

queue
quiescent

R

racist	refer	remittance
rapport	reference	remunerate
readily	referred	rendezvous
readjustment	regrettable	repetition
receipt	reimbursement	resistance
receivable	relief	restaurant
receive	relieve	reversible
recipe	reluctance	rhythm
recommend	remember	roofs
recurrence	remembrance	

S

sacrilegious	siege	succeed
salable	significant	successful
schedule	similar	succinct
scholastic	simultaneous	superintendent
scrupulous	statute	supersede
secretary	stereotype	supervisory
seize	studying	supplementary
separate	subsequent	surprise
sergeant	subsidiary	susceptible
serviceable	subsistence	sympathize
severely	substantially	synonym
shining	subtle	

T

tactfulness	testimonies	transferred
taxable	thorough	tremendous
technician	through	truly
tedious	tournament	twelfth
temperament	tragedy	tying
temporarily	transfer	typical
tendency	transferable	

U

ultimately	underrate	until
umbrella	undoubtedly	usable
unanimity	unforeseen	useful
unbelievable	unnecessary	

V

vacancy	vetoes	vigorous
vacuum	vice versa	vivacious
vague	vicious	voluntary
vehicle	vigilant	

W

waive	weigh	wholly
warranted	weird	witnessed
Wednesday		

Y

yield

Z

zeros
zoology

AGREEMENT OF SUBJECT AND VERB

If	Then	Example
names of books or magazine, or titles of articles	they are considered singular	*Consumer Guides* is published throughout the world.
names of companies or institutions, as a concept	they are singular	Sanders and Rosen, a successful accounting firm, was founded before I was born.
as a plural subject	they are plural	Sanders and Rosen, certified public accountants, have prepared my tax returns.
compound subject	takes a plural verb	The reaction and evaluation of each candidate have been assessed.
compound subject joined by *or* or *nor*	the verb agrees with the subject nearer to it	Neither the ducks nor the duckling is eating the bread. Either the child or her parents are bringing the present.

prepositional phrase separates subject from verb	the verb still agrees with the subject	One of his difficulties was his lack of attention.
each, any, every, one, none, everyone, or either acts as subject	the verb and accompanying pronoun are singular	Each of the women is planning her retirement.
	(None, when construed as *not any,* may be plural)	None of the boys is able to tie his own shoelaces.
		None of the employees are here.
here or there begin sentence	the subject usually follows and agrees with the predicate	Here is the latest manual. There are the two books you wanted.
you use "as well as"	the phrase doesn't affect plurality	The manager, as well as the workers, feels sure the rule is unfair.
you refer to time, amounts, or numbers	plurality depends on use	Three days isn't enough time to complete the work.
		The $8,000 is to be repaid next year.
		These past four months have been rewarding.
you use "a number"	it takes a plural verb	A number of people are here.
you use "the number"	use a singular verb	The number of people present was small.

PREPOSITIONAL PHRASES

agree on something—We agreed on a plan.
agree to something—We agreed to the rule.
agree with person or idea—We agreed with Mark's idea.

angry at or about something
angry with someone

compare to something similar
compare with by considering differences

differ from something else
differ with someone
different from something else

identical to someone
identical with something

similar to

speak to someone—tell
speak with someone—have a conversation

PLURALS

Singular	Plural
addendum	addenda
alumna (female)	alumnae
alumnus (male)	alumni (male or both)
analysis	analyses
appendix	appendixes
basis	bases
crisis	crises
criterion	criteria
datum or data	data
medium	media
parenthesis	parentheses
phenomenon	phenomena

CAPITALIZATION

New York State	her uncle
the state of New York	eastern coastal area
our Madison Avenue branch	southern Illinois
the Orient	Middle East
in oriental lands	north side of the street
the federal government	North Dakota
the Department of Labor	the South
the mid-seventies	East Third Street
the tenth of September	the spring
Acme Trust Company	the spring term
our company	the black people
members of the board of directors	a Negro man
Board of Directors of Smith Company	my mother's house
Uncle Sam	I asked Mother

In titles of books, articles, and so on, capitalize the first and last words and all nouns, verbs, pronouns, adjectives, and adverbs, no matter how short. Capitalize prepositions of four or more letters. Do not capitalize conjunctions (unless they come first or last).

> Just Between You and Me
> Up the Down Staircase

Use italics (or underscoring by hand or on a typewriter) for titles of books, plays, newspapers, magazines, or other long works. Use quotations marks for titles of articles, poems, chapters of books, and parts of longer works.

172

VERB FORMS

Present Tense	Past Tense	Past Participle
arise	arose	arisen
begin	began	begun
bite	bit	bitten
break	broke	broken
burst	burst	burst
choose	chose	chosen
deal	dealt	dealt
dive	dived	dived
drink	drank	drunk
drown	drowned	drowned
eat	ate	eaten
fly	flew	flown
forget	forgot	forgotten (forgot)
get	got	got (gotten)
go	went	gone
hang [object]	hung	hung
hang [person]	hanged	hanged
lay [object]	laid	laid
lead	led	led
lend	lent	lent
lie [person]	lay	lain
lie	lied	lied
loose	loosed	loosed
lose	lost	lost
pay	paid	paid
prove	proved	proved
ride	rode	ridden
rise	rose	risen
swim	swam	swum

take	took	taken
tear	tore	torn
wear	wore	worn
wring	wrung	wrung
write	wrote	written

NUMBERS

If	Then	Example
one through ten	spell out	Only four children came.
higher than ten	use figures	At least 14 students passed.
mixed high and low	be consistent	I bought 4 rolls and 13 pieces of pie for the party.
numbers beginning sentences	spell out	One hundred and six people attended.
numbers representing numbers	use figures	The vote was 7 to 4.
units of measure or in sequence		His score was 75. It measured 3 inches. Look for Figure 6 on page 22.
ordinals: one or two words	spell out	This is the forty-second time I've tried it.
longer than two words	use figures	This is our 103rd try this year.
street names through tenth	spell out	She lives on Second Avenue. She lives at 210 East 42 Street.

If	Then	Example
numbers for dates or streets	don't use "th" or "st"	June 21, not June 21st East 75 Street, not 75th Street *but:* the 99th time

PROBLEMS WITH PUNCTUATION

Type	If you	Then	Example
Comma	join subject and simple predicate	don't separate with a comma	Wrong: The manager of a busy office or even a quiet one, must work hard.
			Right: The manager of a busy office or even a quiet one must work hard.
	have compound subject or predicate	don't separate with a comma	Wrong: Your insurance forms, book, and bulletin, should be placed in your drawer.
			Wrong: Company policies are being written, and will soon reflect the needs of the workers.

Type	If you	Then	Example
Comma	use *and, but, or, for, nor, so,* or *yet* to join independent clauses	use a comma before the linking word unless the clauses are short and closely related	Costs are rising, and the new budget will have to reflect this trend. I warned her about being late, but she paid no attention to me.
	interrupt a main clause with an extra word or phrase	set the word or phrase off with commas (both sides)	She felt, however, that the time was right. It is, as I said before, too early to judge.
	uses nonrestrictive, descriptive clauses or phrases	set them off with commas	*Gone With The Wind,* which I just finished, was fine reading. The temperature, which has been rising all day, has just set a record. Mark Stevens, sitting on the dais next to Susan, is our team captain.

use restrictive, essential clauses or phrases	don't use commas	All the people who hated the music left the hall. Shakespeare's play *Hamlet* raises questions. The condition causing her discomfort has a strange name.
use an adverbial clause (beginning with *when, since, although, as, if, because,* etc.) at the beginning of the sentence	separate it from the main clause with a comma	After you call your office, look for your missing book. Since he was late for work six times, he was fired.
use an adverbial clause following the main clause	use no comma unless it marks a change in thought	He was not hired because he failed the test. You won't be invited if you don't do the work. Production levels are slow this year, although we should see improvement this month.

Type	If you	Then	Example
Comma	begin a sentence with an introductory phrase	use commas to separate it from the rest of the sentence unless it is short	After years of hard work, he was finally promoted.
			In January I'll get my diploma.
	use multiple adjectives to modify the same noun	separate them with a comma (you should be able to reverse the adjectives and insert "and" between them), but omit the comma if the last adjective acts as a unit with the noun	She wore an elegant, graceful dress.
			The cold, chilling days of winter were hard on him.
			He was an angry young man.
	use related, antithetical phrases	separate them with a comma	The more you eat, the fatter you become.
			She was an office worker, not a student.

	use just the month and the year	don't use a comma between them	He'll complete the project in July 1985.
	address someone directly	set the name off with commas	I think, John, we should talk about the schedule.
			Mr. Brown, let's talk about it.
			Let's talk about it, Mr. Brown.
Hyphen	use two or more words as a unit to modify a noun or a pronoun	hyphenate them when they come before the word they modify	He was a bad-tempered person.
			This is first-rate merchandise.
			The fast-moving car went over the cliff.
			but
			She was narrow minded.
			This haircut has been long needed.

Type	If you	Then	Example
Hyphen	use compound noun of any number of parts	use a hyphen or hyphens	brother-in-law great-uncle take-off go-between
	use a prefix with a common word not capitalized	don't hyphenate	unimportant undertake unarmed nonessential
	use a prefix with a capitalized word	hyphenate	anti-German un-American
	write out compound numerals from twenty-one to ninety-nine	hyphenate	forty-seven
	join a number and a unit of measurement to form a modifier	hyphenate	a 5-year plan a two-inch hem a 45-hour week
	use "ex" or "self" before a word	hyphenate (note exception)	ex-president self-respect *but* excommunicate

	use a series of compound modifiers	hyphenate as shown	He used a two- or three-inch margin. We joined a group of four- and five-year-olds.
Semicolon	join independent clauses with no linking word	put a semicolon between them if they are related	Supervisors shouldn't talk down to employees; such behavior is harmful.
	join independent clauses with a linking word longer than three letters (consequently, however, moreover, thus, accordingly, besides)	use a semicolon	Her work habits were consistently poor; however, her boss valued her intelligence. She lost the papers; thus, she spent the day looking for them.
Quotation Marks	name a "term" or "word" or "expression"	enclose the named item in quotation marks	The term "male chauvinist pig" has caught on. The word "pseudonym" is hard to spell.

Type	If you	Then	Example
Quotation Marks	quote someone's words	enclose them in quotation marks	He said, "You'll feel better about it tomorrow."
	refer to someone's words indirectly	don't use quotation marks	She asked why I had come in early.
Apostrophe	show possession	use apostrophe	He ripped the book's cover.
			These are the secretaries' books.
			Bess's land.
			The dog wagged its tail.
			Charles's car.
			but
			The book is hers.
	use plurals	don't use apostrophe	His conditions of acceptance were hard to accept.
			I knew him during the 1970s.

Punctuation with Quotations		
use a comma or period after the quote	put it inside the quote	Yesterday I read the poem "Daybreak." He worked on the show "Soil," but he didn't get credit.
use a semicolon, question mark, or exclamation mark	put it outside the quote	Did he say, "I won't do it"? *but* He shouted, "I won't do it!"

AMACOM EXECUTIVE BOOKS—Paperbacks

John Fenton	The A To Z Of Sales Management	$ 7.95
Hank Seiden	Advertising Pure And Simple	$ 5.95
Alice G. Sargent	The Androgynous Manager	$10.95
John D. Arnold	The Art Of Decision Making	$ 6.95
Oxenfeldt & Miller & Dickinson	A Basic Approach To Executive Decision Making	$ 7.95
Curtis W. Symonds	Basic Financial Management	$ 5.95
William R. Osgood	Basics Of Successful Business Planning	$ 8.95
Ken Cooper	Bodybusiness	$ 5.95
Richard R. Conarroe	Bravely, Bravely In Business	$ 3.95
Jones & Trentin	Budgeting	$12.95
Adam Starchild	Building Wealth	$ 7.95
Laura Brill	Business Writing Quick And Easy	$ 5.95
Rinella & Robbins	Career Power	$ 7.95
Andrew H. Souerwine	Career Strategies	$ 7.95
Donna N. Douglass	Choice And Compromise	$ 8.95
Philip R. Lund	Compelling Selling	$ 5.95
Joseph M. Vles	Computer Basics	$ 6.95
Hart & Schleicher	A Conference And Workshop Planner's Manual	$15.95
Leon Wortman	A Deskbook Of Business Management	$14.95
John D. Drake	Effective Interviewing	$ 7.95
James J. Cribbin	Effective Managerial Leadership	$ 6.95
Eugene J. Benge	Elements Of Modern Management	$ 5.95
Edward N. Rausch	Financial Management For Small Business	$ 7.95
Loren B. Belker	The First-Time Manager	$ 6.95
Ronald D. Brown	From Selling To Managing	$ 5.95
Murray L. Weidenbaum	The Future Of Business Regulation	$ 5.95
Charles Hughes	Goal Setting	$ 4.95
Richard E. Byrd	A Guide To Personal Risk Taking	$ 4.95
Charles Margerison	How To Assess Your Managerial Style	$ 6.95
S.H. Simmons	How To Be The Life Of The Podium	$ 8.95
German D. & German J.	How To Find A Job When Jobs Are Hard To Find	$ 7.95
W.H. Krause	How To Get Started As A Manafuactuer's Representative	$ 8.95
J. Humble	How To Manage By Objectives	$ 4.95
Sal T. Massimino	How To Master The Art Of Closing Sales	$ 5.95
William A. Delaney	How To Run A Growing Company	$ 6.95
J. Douglas Brown	The Human Nature Of Organizations	$ 3.95
Ernest C. Miller	Human Resources Management	$10.95